Welcome to

ROMEO & JULIET Online

This is your Personal Playscript. Like a professional actor's or director's "working script," it has been designed not just to be read, but to be underlined, highlighted, and written in as you explore the play. Feel free to mark it up and make it yours. See page iv for ten ways you can use the Playscript.

Go online for the rich content and tools described on the inside front cover. These will help you understand the script, experience the play in various multimedia formats, and think deeply about the characters and ideas.

Registering for *Romeo & Juliet Online* is easy. See the inside back cover for instructions and your Online Registration Code.

OXFORD
UNIVERSITY PRESS

8 Sampson Mews, Suite 204, Don Mills, Ontario M3C 0H5
www.oupcanada.com

Oxford University Press is a department of the University of Oxford.
It furthers the University's objective of excellence in research, scholarship,
and education by publishing worldwide in

Oxford   New York
Auckland Cape Town Dar es Salaam Hong Kong Karachi
Kuala Lumpur Madrid Melbourne Mexico City Nairobi
New Delhi Shanghai Taipei Toronto

With offices in
Argentina Austria Brazil Chile Czech Republic France Greece
Guatemala Hungary Italy Japan Poland Portugal Singapore
South Korea Switzerland Thailand Turkey Ukraine Vietnam

Oxford is a trade mark of Oxford University Press
in the UK and in certain other countries

Published in Canada
by Oxford University Press

ISBN 978-0-19-544007-2

Oxford University Press is committed to our environment. This book is printed on Forest
Stewardship Council certified paper harvested from a responsibly managed forest.

Mixed Sources
Product group from well-managed
forests and other controlled sources
www.fsc.org Cert no. SW-COC-000952
© 1996 Forest Stewardship Council
FSC

Printed and bound in Canada.

1 2 3 4 — 14 13 12 11

Contents

Ten Tips for Using Your Playscript

Here are ten ways that you can use the Playscript when you are working on staging a scene with your classmates.

1 Underline your character's lines with a pencil. (A pencil is better than a pen or a highlighter because your lines might change as you work with your partner or in your group.)

2 Draw a diagram of the stage, so that everyone is clear where the audience is.

3 Record stage directions. Shakespeare used hardly any stage directions—so you can add these as you work on your scenes. It's important to do this so that you don't forget these details when you come back to rehearse a second time. You'll also want to record the **blocking**—which is the physical movement that you and your group decide on (e.g. "Juliet leans towards Romeo, then quickly turns away and walks downstage left").

4 Record stage business as well. As you work in your group, you will find things to do that will keep the audience interested. Record these ideas so that you don't forget them (e.g., "The Nurse makes funny faces behind Lady Capulet's back").

5 Cut or edit the script. You might decide to cut certain lines. If you do, just put a slash through that part of the script.

6 Sketch an impression. You might want to sketch how you envision the characters or how they might dress.

7 Collect fabric swatches. You might attach a couple of fabric swatches to the playscript to show your group members how you envision a character's costume.

8 Make a list of props that are needed to make the scene more interesting.

9 Jot down the problem that each character is encountering in the scene. What does each character do? How will the character deal with the problem?

10 Go over your lines. Once your lines are set, you can use the Personal Playscript to go over and over your lines until you know them by heart.

Check out the following pages to see what your Playscript might look like once you start working with the text. But remember, these are just a few ideas. Use your imagination to make this Personal Playscript your own. We hope that your copy becomes a slightly tattered and marked-up memento of your journey through the play.

Sample Marked-up Pages

The Balcony Scene (Act 2, Scene 2)

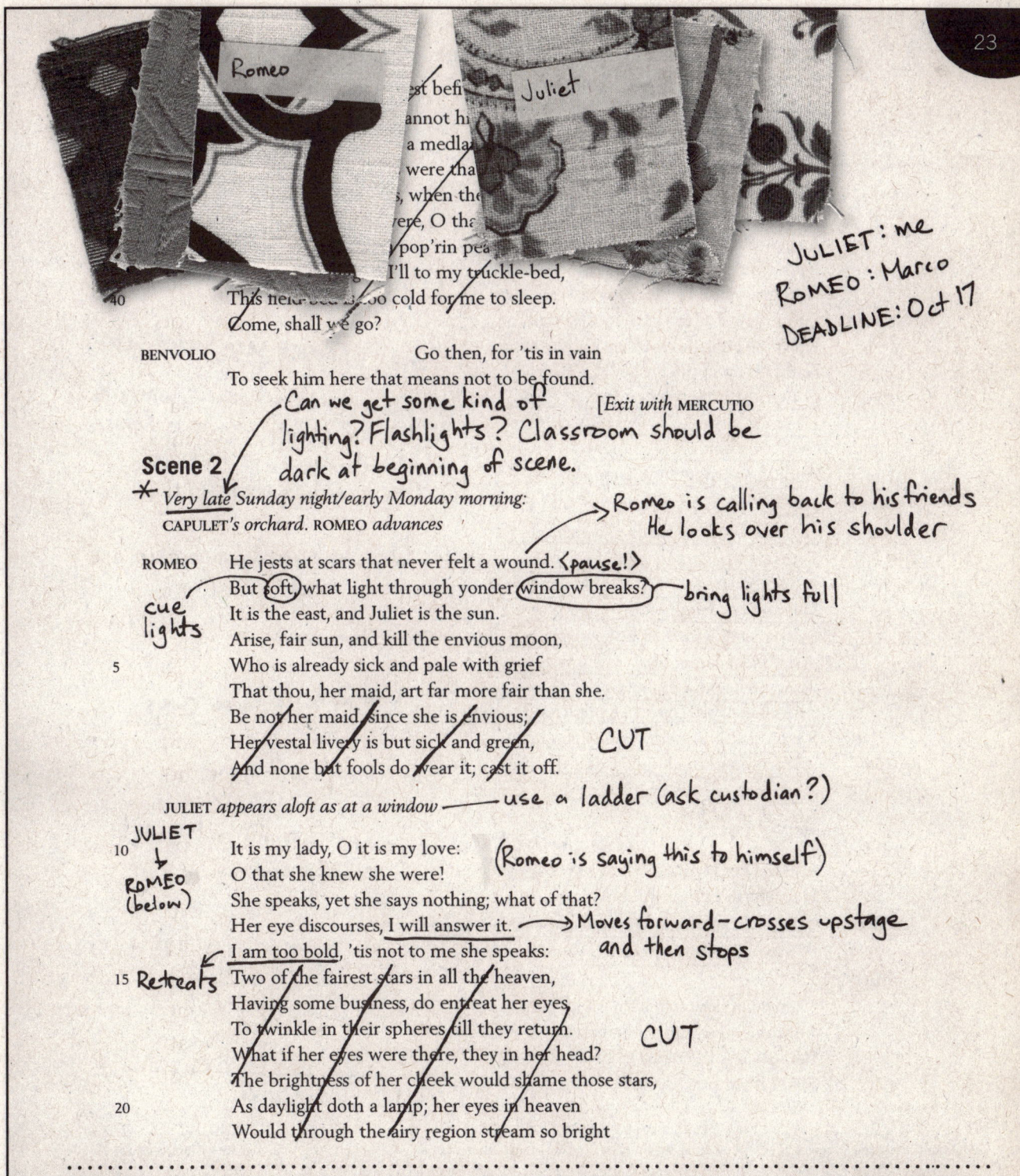

Romeo

Juliet

JULIET: me
ROMEO: Marco
DEADLINE: Oct 17

...est bef...
...annot hi...
a medla...
...were tha...
...when the...
...ere, O tha...
...pop'rin pea...
...I'll to my truckle-bed,

40 This ne... ...oo cold for me to sleep.
Come, shall we go?

BENVOLIO   Go then, for 'tis in vain
To seek him here that means not to be found.

Can we get some kind of lighting? Flashlights? Classroom should be dark at beginning of scene.

[*Exit with* MERCUTIO

Scene 2

* *Very late Sunday night/early Monday morning:*
CAPULET's *orchard.* ROMEO *advances*

→ *Romeo is calling back to his friends He looks over his shoulder*

ROMEO   He jests at scars that never felt a wound. ⟨pause!⟩
cue lights   But soft, what light through yonder window breaks?   *bring lights full*
It is the east, and Juliet is the sun.
Arise, fair sun, and kill the envious moon,
5   Who is already sick and pale with grief
That thou, her maid, art far more fair than she.
Be not her maid, since she is envious;
Her vestal livery is but sick and green,   **CUT**
And none but fools do wear it; cast it off.

JULIET *appears aloft as at a window* ——— *use a ladder (ask custodian?)*

10 JULIET ↓ ROMEO (below)
It is my lady, O it is my love:
O that she knew she were!   *(Romeo is saying this to himself)*
She speaks, yet she says nothing; what of that?
Her eye discourses, I will answer it. → *Moves forward—crosses upstage and then stops*
Retreats   I am too bold, 'tis not to me she speaks:
15   Two of the fairest stars in all the heaven,
Having some business, do entreat her eyes
To twinkle in their spheres till they return.   **CUT**
What if her eyes were there, they in her head?
The brightness of her cheek would shame those stars,
20   As daylight doth a lamp; her eyes in heaven
Would through the airy region stream so bright

---

34 medlar tree A kind of tree with fruit similar to small apples.

38 pop'rin pear A type of pear; also a slang term for a penis.

39 truckle-bed A small bed that could be stored under a larger bed.

2 But soft but wait

8 vestal livery Clothes worn by priestesses of Diana, the moon goddess.

8 sick and green Young girls were prone to "greensickness" (anemia)

9 none but fools do wear it Romeo is comparing the suit worn by followers of Diana (i.e., virgins) to the green-and-yellow uniform of a clown.

13 Her eye discourses her eyes speak volumes

17 in their spheres in their orbit

That birds would sing and think it were not night. *CUT*

See how she leans her cheek upon her hand!

O that I were a glove upon that hand,

Juliet sighs and opens a book, hand on cheek

25   That I might touch that cheek!

JULIET   Ay me!

ROMEO   [*Aside*]   She speaks.   *(whisper)*

O speak again, bright angel, for thou art

As glorious to this night, being o'er my head,

As is a winged messenger of heaven

Unto the white-upturned wond'ring eyes   *CUT*

30   Of mortals that fall back to gaze on him,

When he bestrides the lazy puffing clouds,

And sails upon the bosom of the air.

JULIET   O Romeo, Romeo, wherefore art thou Romeo?

NOTE! I haven't seen Romeo yet

↳ This line is not about where he is but I am asking why he is Romeo (a Montague) and therefore my family's enemy

Deny thy father and refuse thy name;

35   Or if thou wilt not, be but sworn my love,

And I'll no longer be a Capulet.

ROMEO   [*Aside*] Shall I hear more, or shall I speak at this?

JULIET   'Tis but thy name that is my enemy;

Thou art thyself, though not a Montague. ← *begin to come down ladder (1 rung)*

40   What's Montague? It is nor hand nor foot,

Nor arm nor face, nor any other part

Belonging to a man. O be some other name! *really forcefully*

What's in a name? That which we call a rose

By any other word would smell as sweet; ← *come down 2 more rungs*

45   So Romeo would, were he not Romeo call'd,

Retain that dear perfection which he owes

pause → Without that title. Romeo, doff thy name, ← *jump off last rung*

And for thy name, which is no part of thee,

Take all myself.

ROMEO   I take thee at thy word: ——— *Spin around and shriek in surprise*

50   Call me but love, and I'll be new baptis'd;

Henceforth I never will be Romeo.

JULIET   What man art thou that thus bescreen'd in night

So stumblest on my counsel?

ROMEO   By a name

I know not how to tell thee who I am.

55   My name, dear saint, is hateful to myself,

Because it is an enemy to thee;

Had I it written, I would tear the word.

light

ladder

audience

---

28 **winged messenger** angel

31 **bestrides** rides

33 **wherefore** why

34 **Deny thy father...name** forget your family and reject your own name (i.e., Montague)

39 **Thou art thyself...Montague** you would still be yourself if you weren't a Montague

46 **owes** owns

47 **doff** throw off

48 **for thy name** in exchange for giving up your name

50 **Call me but love** just say you'll be my love

52 **bescreen'd** hidden

53 **counsel** private conversation

ACT 2 Scene 2

JULIET   My ears have yet not drunk a hundred words
          Of thy tongue's uttering, yet I know the sound.
60   Art thou not Romeo, and a Montague?

Play it as if she really does not want to know the truth!

ROMEO   Neither, fair maid, if either thee dislike.

What is the subtext? What is she really feeling?

JULIET   How cam'st thou hither, tell me, and wherefore?
          The orchard walls are high and hard to climb,
          And the place death, (considering who thou art,)
65   If any of my kinsmen find thee here.

say under breath

ROMEO   With love's light wings did I o'erperch these walls,
          For stony limits cannot hold love out,
          And what love can do, that dares love attempt:
          Therefore thy kinsmen are no stop to me.

70 JULIET If they do see thee, they will murder thee.

play it really scared and emotional (Maybe we can get another group to do a menacing tableau!)

ROMEO   Alack, there lies more peril in thine eye
          Than twenty of their swords. Look thou but sweet,
          And I am proof against their enmity.

JULIET   I would not for the world they saw thee here.

really mean it! (try pushing him away)

75 ROMEO I have night's cloak to hide me from their eyes,
          And but thou love me, let them find me here;
          My life were better ended by their hate,
          Than death prorogued, wanting of thy love.

JULIET   By whose direction found'st thou out this place?

confront/get really close

80 ROMEO By Love, that first did prompt me to enquire:
          He lent me counsel, and I lent him eyes.
          I am no pilot, yet wert thou as far
          As that vast shore wash'd with the farthest sea,
          I should adventure for such merchandise.

85 JULIET Thou knowest the mask of night is on my face,

(embarrassed)

          Else would a maiden blush bepaint my cheek
          For that which thou hast heard me speak tonight.

gesture with hand

          Fain would I dwell on form, fain, fain deny

gets frustrated and angry

          What I have spoke, but farewell compliment.
90   Dost thou love me? I know thou wilt say 'Ay';

pause

wait before I say this line

          And I will take thy word; yet if thou swear'st,
          Thou mayst prove false: at lovers' perjuries
          They say Jove laughs. O gentle Romeo,
          If thou dost love, pronounce it faithfully;
95   Or if thou think'st I am too quickly won,
          I'll frown and be perverse, and say thee nay,
          So thou wilt woo, but else not for the world.

What is Romeo doing as I speak? we have to figure this out

58 My ears have yet not drunk I haven't even heard you speak

61 if either thee dislike if you don't like either of them

62 How cam'st thou hither how did you get here

66 o'erperch fly over

72 Look thou but sweet look at me kindly

73 I am proof against their enmity they can never hurt me (proof: protected)

76 but unless

77–78 My life were…prorogued if you don't love me, I'd rather they killed me now, than put off death to a later date

84 I should adventure for such merchandise I would dare to travel that far to find you

88 Fain would I dwell on form I would happily observe the rules of politeness and proper behaviour

89 but farewell compliment but it's too late for that

92 perjuries lies

93 Jove Jupiter, the Roman god of oath-taking, thunder, and the sky.

96 perverse difficult

96 say thee nay refuse you

97 So thou wilt woo if you will keep chasing me

Characters in the Play

MONTAGUES

MONTAGUE	Head of the Montague family, and Romeo's father.
LADY MONTAGUE	Romeo's mother.
ROMEO	Teenage son of Lord and Lady Montague.
BENVOLIO	Romeo's cousin. Close friend to both Mercutio and Romeo.
ABRAM	A servant in the Montague household.
BALTHASAR	Romeo's personal servant.

CAPULETS

CAPULET	Head of the Capulet family, and Juliet's father.
LADY CAPULET	Juliet's mother and Tybalt's aunt.
JULIET	Thirteen-year-old daughter of Lord and Lady Capulet.
COUSIN CAPULET	A relative of Capulet; also referred to as "uncle Capulet."
TYBALT	Juliet's cousin and Lady Capulet's nephew.
NURSE	A servant in the Capulet household.
PETER	The Nurse's servant.
SAMPSON GREGORY	Servants in the Capulet household.

PRINCE ESCALES	The Prince of Verona; related to both Paris and Mercutio.
MERCUTIO	Friend of Romeo and Benvolio; related to Prince Escales.
COUNTY PARIS	A nobleman who wishes to marry Juliet; related to Prince Escales.

FRIAR LAWRENCE	A Franciscan friar; friend to both Romeo and Juliet.
FRIAR JOHN	Another Franciscan friar.
AN APOTHECARY	A druggist who sells herbs and medicines in Mantua.
THE CHORUS	A character who acts as a narrator.
THREE MUSICIANS	

Citizens of Verona, masquers, pages, servants, watchmen

Except for Act 5, Scene 1, the action of the play takes place in VERONA

The Prologue

Enter Chorus

Two households, both alike in dignity,
In fair Verona (where we lay our scene),
From ancient grudge break to new mutiny,
Where civil blood makes civil hands unclean.
5   From forth the fatal loins of these two foes
A pair of star-cross'd lovers take their life;
Whose misadventur'd piteous overthrows
Doth with their death bury their parents' strife.
The fearful passage of their death-mark'd love,
10 And the continuance of their parents' rage,
Which but their children's end nought could remove,
Is now the two hours' traffic of our stage;
The which if you with patient ears attend,
What here shall miss, our toil shall strive to mend.

[Exit

ACT 1   Scene 1

Sunday morning: a public place. Enter SAMPSON *and* GREGORY,
with swords and bucklers, of the house of Capulet

SAMPSON   Gregory, on my word, we'll not carry coals.

GREGORY   No, for then we should be colliers.

SAMPSON   I mean, and we be in choler, we'll draw.

GREGORY   Ay, while you live, draw your neck out of collar.

5   SAMPSON   I strike quickly, being moved.

GREGORY   But thou art not quickly moved to strike.

SAMPSON   A dog of the house of Montague moves me.

GREGORY   To move is to stir, and to be valiant is to stand: therefore
if thou art moved thou runn'st away.

10 SAMPSON   A dog of that house shall move me to stand: I will take
the wall of any man or maid of Montague's.

GREGORY   That shows thee a weak slave, for the weakest goes to the
wall.

SAMPSON   'Tis true, and therefore women being the weaker vessels
15   are ever thrust to the wall: therefore I will push
Montague's men from the wall, and thrust his maids to
the wall.

---

3 mutiny violence

4 civil blood … unclean citizens stain their hands with the blood of their fellow citizens

6 star-cross'd doomed

7 misadventur'd piteous overthrows unfortunate accidents

9 fearful passage frightening course

11 but their children's … remove only their children's deaths could stop

12 the two hours' traffic of our stage our subject for the next two hours

14 What here shall miss what is missing from this Prologue

0 s.d. bucklers small shields

1 carry coals take an insult

2 colliers coal men (considered of low social status)

3 choler anger

3 draw draw our swords

4 collar the hangman's noose

8 stand stay and fight

10–11 take the wall of show myself to be better than

12–13 the weakest goes to the wall the weaker opponent gives way to the stronger

	GREGORY	The quarrel is between our masters, and us their men.
	SAMPSON	'Tis all one, I will show myself a tyrant: when I have
20		fought with the men, I will be civil with the maids; I will
		cut off their heads.
	GREGORY	The heads of the maids?
	SAMPSON	Ay, the heads of the maids, or their maidenheads, take it
		in what sense thou wilt.
25	GREGORY	They must take it in sense that feel it.
	SAMPSON	Mé they shall feel while I am able to stand, and 'tis
		known I am a pretty piece of flesh.
	GREGORY	'Tis well thou art not fish; if thou hadst, thou hadst been
		poor-John. Draw thy tool, here comes of the house of
30		Montagues.

Enter two SERVINGMEN, ABRAM *and* BALTHASAR

	SAMPSON	My naked weapon is out. Quarrel, I will back thee.
	GREGORY	How, turn thy back and run?
	SAMPSON	Fear me not.
	GREGORY	No, marry, I fear thee!
35	SAMPSON	Let us take the law of our sides, let them begin.
	GREGORY	I will frown as I pass by, and let them take it as they list.
	SAMPSON	Nay, as they dare. I will bite my thumb at them, which is
		disgrace to them if they bear it.
	ABRAM	Do you bite your thumb at us, sir?
40	SAMPSON	I do bite my thumb, sir.
	ABRAM	Do you bite your thumb at us, sir?
	SAMPSON	[*Aside to* GREGORY] Is the law of our side if I say ay?
	GREGORY	[*Aside to* SAMPSON] No.
	SAMPSON	No, sir, I do not bite my thumb at you, sir, but I bite my
45		thumb, sir.
	GREGORY	Do you quarrel, sir?
	ABRAM	Quarrel, sir? No, sir.
	SAMPSON	But if you do, sir, I am for you. I serve as good a man as
		you.
50	ABRAM	No better.
	SAMPSON	Well, sir.

Enter BENVOLIO

· ·

19 'Tis all one it makes no difference

23 maidenheads virginities

24 in what sense however

25 in sense sensually

27 a pretty piece of flesh an attractive fellow

29 poor-John dried salted fish (associated with a lack of sex drive)

29 tool weapon

31 back support

34 marry indeed

35 take the law of our sides keep within the law

36 list like

37 bite my thumb at them make a rude gesture

48 I am for you I am ready for you

GREGORY [*Aside to* SAMPSON] Say 'better', here comes one of my
                   master's kinsmen.

SAMPSON Yes, better, sir.

55 ABRAM You lie.

SAMPSON Draw, if you be men. Gregory, remember thy washing
                   blow.

They fight

BENVOLIO Part, fools!
                   Put up your swords, you know not what you do.

Beats down their swords

Enter TYBALT

60 TYBALT What, art thou drawn among these heartless hinds?
                   Turn thee, Benvolio, look upon thy death.

BENVOLIO I do but keep the peace. Put up thy sword,
                   Or manage it to part these men with me.

TYBALT What, drawn and talk of peace? I hate the word,
65   As I hate hell, all Montagues, and thee.
                   Have at thee, coward.

They fight

*Enter several of both houses, who join the fray, and
three or four* CITIZENS *as* OFFICERS *of the Watch, with
clubs or partisans*

OFFICERS Clubs, bills, and partisans! Strike! Beat them down!
                   Down with the Capulets! Down with the Montagues!

Enter old CAPULET *in his gown, and his wife* LADY CAPULET

CAPULET What noise is this? Give me my long sword, ho!

70 LADY CAPULET A crutch, a crutch! why call you for a sword?

CAPULET My sword, I say! old Montague is come,
                   And flourishes his blade in spite of me.

Enter old MONTAGUE *and his wife* LADY MONTAGUE

MONTAGUE Thou villain Capulet!—Hold me not, let me go.

LADY MONTAGUE Thou shalt not stir one foot to seek a foe.

Enter PRINCE ESCALES *with his train*

- -

56 washing slashing

59 Put up put away

60 heartless hinds cowardly servants;
a reference to a female deer (hind)
without a mate (hart)

62 but only

63 manage it use it

66 Have at thee get ready to fight

67 bills, and partisans Types of
weapons.

68 s.d. gown dressing gown (night
dress)

69 long sword A weapon that was out
of date even in Shakespeare's day.

72 in spite of me to taunt me

75 PRINCE   Rebellious subjects, enemies to peace,
Profaners of this neighbour-stained steel—
Will they not hear?—What ho, you men, you beasts!
That quench the fire of your pernicious rage
With purple fountains issuing from your veins:
80   On pain of torture, from those bloody hands
Throw your mistemper'd weapons to the ground,
And hear the sentence of your moved prince.
Three civil brawls, bred of an airy word,
By thee, old Capulet, and Montague,
85   Have thrice disturb'd the quiet of our streets,
And made Verona's ancient citizens
Cast by their grave beseeming ornaments
To wield old partisans, in hands as old,
Canker'd with peace, to part your canker'd hate;
90   If ever you disturb our streets again,
Your lives shall pay the forfeit of the peace.
For this time all the rest depart away:
You, Capulet, shall go along with me,
And, Montague, come you this afternoon,
95   To know our farther pleasure in this case,
To old Free-town, our common judgement-place.
Once more, on pain of death, all men depart.

        [*Exeunt all but* MONTAGUE, LADY MONTAGUE, *and* BENVOLIO

MONTAGUE Who set this ancient quarrel new abroach?
Speak, nephew, were you by when it began?

100 BENVOLIO Here were the servants of your adversary,
And yours, close fighting ere I did approach:
I drew to part them; in the instant came
The fiery Tybalt, with his sword prepar'd,
Which, as he breath'd defiance to my ears,
105   He swung about his head and cut the winds,
Who, nothing hurt withal, hiss'd him in scorn;
While we were interchanging thrusts and blows,
Came more and more, and fought on part and part,
Till the prince came, who parted either part.

110 LADY MONTAGUE   O where is Romeo? saw you him today?
Right glad I am he was not at this fray.

BENVOLIO Madam, an hour before the worshipp'd sun
Peer'd forth the golden window of the east,
A troubled mind drive me to walk abroad,

. . . .

76 Profaners abusers

76 neighbour-stained steel swords covered in your neighbour's blood

81 mistemper'd bad tempered; poorly made

82 moved angry

83 bred of an airy word started by some offhand remark

87 Cast by their ... ornaments cast off their dignified attire

88 as old as old as the weapons themselves

89 Canker'd rusty

89 canker'd hate corrupting hatred

91 Your lives shall ... peace you will pay with your lives for breaking the peace

98 Who set this ... abroach? who restarted this fight

102 in the instant just then

108 on part and part on either side

109 who parted either part who divided the fighting parties

115 Where underneath the grove of sycamore,
That westward rooteth from this city side,
So early walking did I see your son;
Towards him I made, but he was ware of me,
And stole into the covert of the wood;
120 I, measuring his affections by my own,
Which then most sought where most might not be found,
Being one too many by my weary self,
Pursu'd my humour, not pursuing his,
And gladly shunn'd who gladly fled from me.

125 **MONTAGUE** Many a morning hath he there been seen,
With tears augmenting the fresh morning's dew,
Adding to clouds more clouds with his deep sighs,
But all so soon as the all-cheering sun
Should in the farthest east begin to draw
130 The shady curtains from Aurora's bed,
Away from light steals home my heavy son,
And private in his chamber pens himself,
Shuts up his windows, locks fair daylight out,
And makes himself an artificial night:
135 Black and portentous must this humour prove,
Unless good counsel may the cause remove.

BENVOLIO My noble uncle, do you know the cause?

MONTAGUE I neither know it, nor can learn of him.

BENVOLIO Have you importun'd him by any means?

140 **MONTAGUE** Both by myself and many other friends,
But he, his own affections' counsellor,
Is to himself (I will not say how true)
But to himself so secret and so close,
So far from sounding and discovery,
145 As is the bud bit with an envious worm
Ere he can spread his sweet leaves to the air,
Or dedicate his beauty to the sun.
Could we but learn from whence his sorrows grow,
We would as willingly give cure as know.

Enter ROMEO

150 **BENVOLIO** See where he comes. So please you step aside,
I'll know his grievance or be much denied.

MONTAGUE I would thou wert so happy by thy stay
To hear true shrift. Come, madam, let's away.

. . . .

115 sycamore A type of maple tree, associated with lovers (sick-amor, or "sick-love").

116 That westward rooteth ... side that grows on the west side of this city

118 ware wary

119 covert cover

120 measuring his affections ... own interpreting his feelings by comparing them with my own

123 Pursu'd my humour went where I felt like going

124 gladly shunn'd ... me was happy to avoid talking to him, since he wanted to avoid me anyway

126 augmenting adding to

130 Aurora Roman goddess of dawn.

135 portentous ominous

135 humour mood; state of mind

139 importun'd asked

144 sounding examination

152 I would thou ... stay I hope you will be lucky enough, by staying here

153 shrift confession

[*Exeunt* MONTAGUE *and* LADY MONTAGUE

	BENVOLIO	Good morrow, cousin.
	ROMEO	Is the day so young?
155	BENVOLIO	But new struck nine.
	ROMEO	Ay me, sad hours seem long.
		Was that my father that went hence so fast?
	BENVOLIO	It was. What sadness lengthens Romeo's hours?
	ROMEO	Not having that, which, having, makes them short.
	BENVOLIO	In love?
160	ROMEO	Out—
	BENVOLIO	Of love?
	ROMEO	Out of her favour where I am in love.
	BENVOLIO	Alas that Love, so gentle in his view,
		Should be so tyrannous and rough in proof!
165	ROMEO	Alas that Love, whose view is muffled still,
		Should, without eyes, see pathways to his will!
		Where shall we dine? O me! what fray was here?
		Yet tell me not, for I have heard it all:
		Here's much to do with hate, but more with love:
170		Why then, O brawling love, O loving hate,
		O any thing of nothing first create!
		O heavy lightness, serious vanity,
		Misshapen chaos of well-seeming forms,
		Feather of lead, bright smoke, cold fire, sick health,
175		Still-waking sleep, that is not what it is!
		This love feel I, that feel no love in this.
		Dost thou not laugh?
	BENVOLIO	No, coz, I rather weep.
	ROMEO	Good heart, at what?
	BENVOLIO	At thy good heart's oppression.
	ROMEO	Why, such is love's transgression:
180		Griefs of mine own lie heavy in my breast,
		Which thou wilt propagate to have it press'd
		With more of thine; this love that thou hast shown
		Doth add more grief to too much of mine own.
		Love is a smoke made with the fume of sighs,
185		Being purg'd, a fire sparkling in lovers' eyes,
		Being vex'd, a sea nourish'd with loving tears.
		What is it else? a madness most discreet,

---

154 morrow morning

163 so gentle in his view who looks so gentle

164 tyrannous and rough in proof cruel and unkind in reality

165 muffled still always blindfolded

166 see pathways to his will see ways to make people fall in love

171 of nothing first create created from nothing

172 vanity superficiality; shallowness

173 well-seeming pleasant-looking

175 Still-waking always awake

176 This love feel ... this. this is the kind of love I feel, even though I get no love in return

177 coz cousin

179 such is love's transgression that's the problem with love

181–182 Which thou wilt ... thine which you will increase if you burden me with your own sadness

184 fume breath

185 purg'd made pure

186 vex'd troubled

187 discreet wise

A choking gall, and a preserving sweet.
Farewell, my coz.

BENVOLIO   Soft, I will go along;

190   And if you leave me so, you do me wrong.

ROMEO   Tut, I have lost myself, I am not here,
This is not Romeo, he's some other where.

BENVOLIO   Tell me in sadness, who is that you love?

ROMEO   What, shall I groan and tell thee?

BENVOLIO   Groan? why, no;

195   But sadly tell me, who?

ROMEO   Bid a sick man in sadness make his will—
A word ill urg'd to one that is so ill:
In sadness, cousin, I do love a woman.

BENVOLIO   I aim'd so near, when I suppos'd you lov'd.

200 **ROMEO**   A right good mark-man! and she's fair I love.

BENVOLIO   A right fair mark, fair coz, is soonest hit.

ROMEO   Well, in that hit you miss: she'll not be hit
With Cupid's arrow, she hath Dian's wit;
And in strong proof of chastity well arm'd,

205   From Love's weak childish bow she lives uncharm'd.
She will not stay the siege of loving terms,
Nor bide th'encounter of assailing eyes,
Nor ope her lap to saint-seducing gold.
O, she is rich in beauty, only poor

210   That when she dies, with beauty dies her store.

BENVOLIO   Then she hath sworn that she will still live chaste?

ROMEO   She hath, and in that sparing makes huge waste;
For beauty starv'd with her severity
Cuts beauty off from all posterity.

215   She is too fair, too wise, wisely too fair,
To merit bliss by making me despair.
She hath forsworn to love, and in that vow
Do I live dead, that live to tell it now.

BENVOLIO   Be rul'd by me, forget to think of her.

220 **ROMEO**   O teach me how I should forget to think.

BENVOLIO   By giving liberty unto thine eyes,
Examine other beauties.

ROMEO   'Tis the way
To call hers (exquisite) in question more:

. . . .

188 gall bitterness

188 preserving sweet healing sweetness

189 Soft wait

193 sadness seriousness; misery

200 mark-man archer

201 right fair mark easy target

203 Dian Roman goddess of the moon, the hunt, and chastity.

204 in strong proof ... arm'd protected by the strong armour of chastity

206 stay the siege put up with the assault

207 bide th'encounter endure the attack

210 with beauty dies her store her beauty will die with her

212 sparing saving

214 posterity future generations

215 fair pretty; just

216 merit bliss earn her way to heaven

219 Be rul'd by me take my advice

223 To call...more to examine her beauty, which is exquisite, more closely

These happy masks that kiss fair ladies' brows,
225 Being black, puts us in mind they hide the fair;
He that is strucken blind cannot forget
The precious treasure of his eyesight lost;
Show me a mistress that is passing fair,
What doth her beauty serve but as a note
230 Where I may read who pass'd that passing fair?
Farewell, thou canst not teach me to forget.

BENVOLIO I'll pay that doctrine, or else die in debt.   [*Exeunt*

Scene 2

A street: enter CAPULET, COUNTY PARIS, *and the*
CLOWN, SERVANT *to* CAPULET

CAPULET But Montague is bound as well as I,
In penalty alike, and 'tis not hard, I think,
For men so old as we to keep the peace.

PARIS Of honourable reckoning are you both,
5 And pity 'tis, you liv'd at odds so long.
But now, my lord, what say you to my suit?

CAPULET But saying o'er what I have said before:
My child is yet a stranger in the world,
She hath not seen the change of fourteen years;
10 Let two more summers wither in their pride,
Ere we may think her ripe to be a bride.

PARIS Younger than she are happy mothers made.

CAPULET And too soon marr'd are those so early made.
Earth hath swallow'd all my hopes but she;
15 She's the hopeful lady of my earth.
But woo her, gentle Paris, get her heart,
My will to her consent is but a part;
And she agreed, within her scope of choice
Lies my consent and fair according voice.
20 This night I hold an old accustom'd feast,
Whereto I have invited many a guest,
Such as I love, and you among the store,
One more, most welcome, makes my number more.
At my poor house look to behold this night
25 Earth-treading stars that make dark heaven light.
Such comfort as do lusty young men feel
When well-apparell'd April on the heel

224 happy masks masks worn by fashionable women
228 passing fair very beautiful
230 pass'd surpassed; went beyond
232 I'll pay that ... debt. I'll teach you that I'm right, or die trying
4 reckoning reputation; age
9 She hath not ... years she is not yet fourteen
14 hopes Capulet refers to the fact that all his other children have died.
18 And once
18 within her scope of choice with whoever she chooses
20 accustom'd customary
25 Earth-treading stars beautiful women
27 well-apparell'd well-dressed (i.e., in spring flowers)

Of limping winter treads, even such delight

Among fresh fennel buds shall you this night

30 Inherit at my house; hear all, all see;

And like her most whose merit most shall be;

Which on more view of many, mine, being one,

May stand in number, though in reck'ning none.

Come go with me. [*To* SERVANT] Go, sirrah, trudge about

35 Through fair Verona, find those persons out

Whose names are written there [*Gives a paper*], and to them say,

My house and welcome on their pleasure stay.   [*Exit with* PARIS

SERVANT Find them out whose names are written here! It is

written that the shoemaker should meddle with his yard

40 and the tailor with his last, the fisher with his pencil and

the painter with his nets; but I am sent to find those

persons whose names are here writ, and can never find

what names the writing person hath here writ. I must to

the learned. In good time!

Enter BENVOLIO *and* ROMEO

45 BENVOLIO Tut, man, one fire burns out another's burning,

One pain is lessen'd by another's anguish;

Turn giddy, and be holp by backward turning;

One desperate grief cures with another's languish:

Take thou some new infection to thy eye,

50 And the rank poison of the old will die.

ROMEO Your plantain leaf is excellent for that.

BENVOLIO For what, I pray thee?

ROMEO   For your broken shin.

BENVOLIO Why, Romeo, art thou mad?

ROMEO Not mad, but bound more than a madman is:

55 Shut up in prison, kept without my food,

Whipt and tormented, and—God-den, good fellow.

SERVANT God gi' god-den. I pray, sir, can you read?

ROMEO Ay, mine own fortune in my misery.

SERVANT Perhaps you have learned it without book; but I pray,

60 can you read any thing you see?

ROMEO Ay, if I know the letters and the language.

SERVANT Ye say honestly, rest you merry.

ROMEO Stay, fellow, I can read.

30 Inherit experience

32–33 Which on more … none when you have seen Juliet among other beautiful women, you may (or may not) think she is the most desirable

34 sirrah A title used when addressing those of lower rank.

37 stay await

39 yard A rod used by tailors to measure cloth.

40 last A form used by shoemakers to make shoes.

44 In good time! what good timing

51 plantain leaf A plant used to heal minor wounds.

56 God-den good evening

57 gi' Short for "give you."

59 without book by heart

62 rest you merry good day

He reads the letter

'Signior Martino and his wife and daughters,
65 County Anselme and his beauteous sisters,
The lady widow of Vitruvio,
Signior Placentio and his lovely nieces,
Mercutio and his brother Valentine,
Mine uncle Capulet, his wife and daughters,
70 My fair niece Rosaline, and Livia,
Signior Valentio and his cousin Tybalt,
Lucio and the lively Helena.'
A fair assembly: whither should they come?

SERVANT Up.

75 ROMEO Whither? to supper?

SERVANT To our house.

ROMEO Whose house?

SERVANT My master's.

ROMEO Indeed I should have asked thee that before.

80 SERVANT Now I'll tell you without asking. My master is the great
rich Capulet, and if you be not of the house of
Montagues, I pray come and crush a cup of wine. Rest
you merry.   [*Exit*

BENVOLIO At this same ancient feast of Capulet's
85 Sups the fair Rosaline whom thou so loves,
With all the admired beauties of Verona:
Go thither, and with unattainted eye
Compare her face with some that I shall show,
And I will make thee think thy swan a crow.

90 ROMEO When the devout religion of mine eye
Maintains such falsehood, then turn tears to fires;
And these who, often drown'd, could never die,
Transparent heretics, be burnt for liars.
One fairer than my love! the all-seeing sun
95 Ne'er saw her match since first the world begun.

BENVOLIO Tut, you saw her fair, none else being by,
Herself pois'd with herself in either eye;
But in that crystal scales let there be weigh'd
Your lady's love against some other maid
100 That I will show you shining at this feast,
And she shall scant show well that now seems best.

82 **crush** drink

87 **thither** there
87 **unattainted** uninfected

90–93 **When the devout … liars.** if I
ever claim someone is more beautiful
than Rosaline, may my tears turn to
fire and burn my eyes as if they were
heretics (unbelievers)

98 **crystal scales** Romeo's eyes

ROMEO   I'll go along no such sight to be shown,
But to rejoice in splendour of mine own.   [*Exeunt*

Scene 3

Sunday afternoon: CAPULET's *house. Enter* CAPULET's
WIFE *and* NURSE

LADY CAPULET   Nurse, where's my daughter? call her forth to me.

NURSE   Now by my maidenhead at twelve year old,
I bade her come. What, lamb! What, ladybird!
God forbid, where's this girl? What, Juliet?

Enter JULIET

5   JULIET   How now, who calls?

NURSE   Your mother.

JULIET   Madam, I am here, what is your will?

LADY CAPULET   This is the matter. Nurse, give leave a while,
We must talk in secret. Nurse, come back again,
10   I have remember'd me, thou s' hear our counsel.
Thou knowest my daughter's of a pretty age.

NURSE   Faith, I can tell her age unto an hour.

LADY CAPULET   She's not fourteen.

NURSE   I'll lay fourteen of my teeth—
And yet to my teen be it spoken, I have but four—
15   She's not fourteen. How long is it now
To Lammas-tide?

LADY CAPULET   A fortnight and odd days.

NURSE   Even or odd, of all days in the year,
Come Lammas-eve at night shall she be fourteen.
Susan and she—God rest all Christian souls!—
20   Were of an age. Well, Susan is with God,
She was too good for me. But as I said,
On Lammas-eve at night shall she be fourteen,
That shall she, marry, I remember it well.
'Tis since the earthquake now aleven years,
25   And she was wean'd—I never shall forget it—
Of all the days of the year, upon that day;
For I had then laid wormwood to my dug,
Sitting in the sun under the dove-house wall.

- -

2 maidenhead virginity

8 give leave leave us alone

10 thou s' you shall

10 counsel private conversation

13 lay bet

14 teen sorrow

16 Lammas-tide Lady Mass (August harvest festival)

16 fortnight two weeks

19 Susan The Nurse's daughter who died at a young age.

20 of an age the same age

27 wormwood A bitter-tasting plant, used to discourage infants from suckling.

27 dug breast

My lord and you were then at Mantua—

30 Nay, I do bear a brain—but as I said,
When it did taste the wormwood on the nipple
Of my dug, and felt it bitter, pretty fool,
To see it tetchy and fall out wi'th'dug!
'Shake!' quoth the dove-house; 'twas no need, I trow,

35 To bid me trudge.
And since that time it is aleven years,
For then she could stand high-lone; nay, by th'rood,
She could have run and waddled all about;
For even the day before, she broke her brow,

40 And then my husband—God be with his soul,
'A was a merry man—took up the child.
'Yea', quoth he, 'dost thou fall upon thy face?
Thou wilt fall backward when thou hast more wit,
Wilt thou not, Jule?' And by my holidam,

45 The pretty wretch left crying, and said 'Ay'.
To see now how a jest shall come about!
I warrant, and I should live a thousand years,
I never should forget it: 'Wilt thou not, Jule?' quoth he,
And, pretty fool, it stinted, and said 'Ay'.

50 **LADY CAPULET**   Enough of this, I pray thee hold thy peace.

NURSE   Yes, madam, yet I cannot choose but laugh,
To think it should leave crying, and say 'Ay':
And yet I warrant it had upon it brow
A bump as big as a young cock'rel's stone,

55 A perilous knock, and it cried bitterly.
'Yea', quoth my husband, 'fall'st upon thy face?
Thou wilt fall backward when thou comest to age,
Wilt thou not, Jule?' It stinted, and said 'Ay'.

JULIET   And stint thou too, I pray thee, Nurse, say I.

60 **NURSE**   Peace, I have done. God mark thee to his grace,
Thou wast the prettiest babe that e'er I nurs'd.
And I might live to see thee married once,
I have my wish.

LADY CAPULET   Marry, that 'marry' is the very theme

65 I came to talk of. Tell me, daughter Juliet,
How stands your dispositions to be married?

JULIET   It is an honour that I dream not of.

NURSE   An honour! were not I thine only nurse,
I would say thou hadst suck'd wisdom from thy teat.

---

30 bear a brain have a good memory
31 it Juliet (as a baby)
33 tetchy fretful; irritated
34 'Shake!' quoth the dove-house the dove-house started shaking (because of the earthquake)

34 I trow I can assure you
35 To bid me trudge to tell me to move
37 high-lone on her own
37 by th'rood by the holy cross

39 broke her brow cut her forehead
44 holidam holy dame ("by the Virgin Mary")
46 come about come true
47 and if
49 stinted stopped crying

54 cock'rel's stone young rooster's testicle
57 comest to age are older
60 God mark thee to his grace God bless you
66 How stands … married? how do you feel about getting married

70 LADY CAPULET Well, think of marriage now; younger than you,
Here in Verona, ladies of esteem,
Are made already mothers. By my count,
I was your mother much upon these years
That you are now a maid. Thus then in brief:
75 The valiant Paris seeks you for his love.

NURSE A man, young lady! lady, such a man
As all the world—Why, he's a man of wax.

LADY CAPULET Verona's summer hath not such a flower.

NURSE Nay, he's a flower, in faith, a very flower.

80 LADY CAPULET What say you, can you love the gentleman?
This night you shall behold him at our feast;
Read o'er the volume of young Paris' face,
And find delight writ there with beauty's pen;
Examine every married lineament,
85 And see how one another lends content;
And what obscur'd in this fair volume lies
Find written in the margent of his eyes.
This precious book of love, this unbound lover,
To beautify him, only lacks a cover.
90 The fish lives in the sea, and 'tis much pride
For fair without the fair within to hide;
That book in many's eyes doth share the glory
That in gold clasps locks in the golden story:
So shall you share all that he doth possess,
95 By having him, making yourself no less.

NURSE No less! nay, bigger women grow by men.

LADY CAPULET Speak briefly, can you like of Paris' love?

JULIET I'll look to like, if looking liking move;
But no more deep will I endart mine eye
100 Than your consent gives strength to make it fly.

Enter SERVINGMAN

SERVINGMAN Madam, the guests are come, supper served up, you
called, my young lady asked for, the Nurse cursed in the
pantry, and every thing in extremity. I must hence to
wait, I beseech you follow straight.   [*Exit*

105 LADY CAPULET We follow thee. Juliet, the County stays.

NURSE Go, girl, seek happy nights to happy days.   [*Exeunt*

. . . .

73–74 much upon these … maid at about your age

77 a man of wax a perfect model of a man

79 in faith for sure

84 married lineament well-matched feature (like illustrations in a book)

85 one another lends content each feature works in harmony with the others (as the lines of a book make up its content)

87 margent margin

88 unbound unmarried (or loose-leaf, without a permanent binding)

90–91 'tis much pride … hide a beautiful book deserves a beautiful cover (i.e., a handsome man deserves a beautiful wife)

96 grow get pregnant

98 I'll look to like I'll do my best to like him

98 if looking liking move if just looking at him can move me to like him

99–100 no more deep … fly I won't shoot him encouraging glances without your consent

103 in extremity in an uproar

105 the County stays Count Paris awaits

Scene 4

Sunday evening: outside CAPULET'*s house. Enter*
ROMEO, MERCUTIO, BENVOLIO, *with five or six other*
MASKERS, TORCH-BEARERS

	ROMEO	What, shall this speech be spoke for our excuse?
		Or shall we on without apology?
	BENVOLIO	The date is out of such prolixity:
		We'll have no Cupid hoodwink'd with a scarf,
5		Bearing a Tartar's painted bow of lath,
		Scaring the ladies like a crow-keeper,
		Nor no without-book prologue, faintly spoke
		After the prompter, for our entrance;
		But let them measure us by what they will,
10		We'll measure them a measure and be gone.
	ROMEO	Give me a torch, I am not for this ambling;
		Being but heavy, I will bear the light.
	MERCUTIO	Nay, gentle Romeo, we must have you dance.
	ROMEO	Not I, believe me. You have dancing shoes
15		With nimble soles, I have a soul of lead
		So stakes me to the ground I cannot move.
	MERCUTIO	You are a lover, borrow Cupid's wings,
		And soar with them above a common bound.
	ROMEO	I am too sore enpierced with his shaft
20		To soar with his light feathers, and so bound
		I cannot bound a pitch above dull woe:
		Under love's heavy burden do I sink.
	MERCUTIO	And to sink in it should you burden love,
		Too great oppression for a tender thing.
25	ROMEO	Is love a tender thing? it is too rough,
		Too rude, too boist'rous, and it pricks like thorn.
	MERCUTIO	If love be rough with you, be rough with love:
		Prick love for pricking, and you beat love down.
		Give me a case to put my visage in, [*Puts on a mask*]
30		A visor for a visor! what care I
		What curious eye doth cote deformities?
		Here are the beetle brows shall blush for me.
	BENVOLIO	Come knock and enter, and no sooner in,
		But every man betake him to his legs.
35	ROMEO	A torch for me: let wantons light of heart

- -

0 s.d. Maskers party-goers wearing masks

1 shall this speech … excuse shall we make a speech to excuse ourselves

3 The date is out of such prolixity long-winded speeches are old-fashioned

4 hoodwink'd blindfolded

5 a Tartar's painted bow of lath a flimsy fake bow (a theatrical prop)

6 crow-keeper scarecrow

7 without-book memorized

10 measure them a measure dance for them

11 ambling horsing around

12 heavy sad (with a pun on "light")

18 above a common bound beyond the limits of the ordinary

20–21 so bound … woe so tied down I can't rise above my sadness

23 And to sink … love if you sink in love, you will disappoint your loved one

28 Prick love for pricking fight back against love's jabs

31 cote notice

32 beetle brows thick heavy eyebrows (on the mask)

35 wantons merry-makers

Tickle the senseless rushes with their heels;
For I am proverb'd with a grandsire phrase,
I'll be a candle-holder and look on:
The game was ne'er so fair, and I am done.

40 MERCUTIO Tut, dun's the mouse, the constable's own word.
If thou art Dun, we'll draw thee from the mire,
Or (save your reverence) love, wherein thou stickest
Up to the ears. Come, we burn daylight, ho!

ROMEO Nay, that's not so.

MERCUTIO   I mean, sir, in delay
45 We waste our lights in vain, like lights by day.
Take our good meaning, for our judgement sits
Five times in that ere once in our five wits.

ROMEO And we mean well in going to this mask,
But 'tis no wit to go.

MERCUTIO   Why, may one ask?

50 ROMEO I dreamt a dream tonight.

MERCUTIO   And so did I.

ROMEO Well, what was yours?

MERCUTIO   That dreamers often lie.

ROMEO In bed asleep, while they do dream things true.

MERCUTIO O then I see Queen Mab hath been with you:
She is the fairies' midwife, and she comes
55 In shape no bigger than an agate-stone
On the forefinger of an alderman,
Drawn with a team of little atomi
Over men's noses as they lie asleep.
Her chariot is an empty hazel-nut,
60 Made by the joiner squirrel or old grub,
Time out a'mind the fairies' coachmakers:
Her waggon-spokes made of long spinners' legs,
The cover of the wings of grasshoppers,
Her traces of the smallest spider web,
65 Her collars of the moonshine's wat'ry beams,
Her whip of cricket's bone, the lash of film,
Her waggoner a small grey-coated gnat,
Not half so big as a round little worm
Prick'd from the lazy finger of a maid.
70 And in this state she gallops night by night
Through lovers' brains, and then they dream of love,

36 Tickle the senseless ... heels dance; kick up the floor-covers with their feet

37 I am proverb'd ... phrase I'll quote the old proverb

39 The game was ... done I'll quit while I am ahead

40 dun's the mouse "keep quiet"

40 the constable's own word Like a watchword a policeman on patrol would use ("Keep quiet!").

41 If thou art ... mire "Dun-in-the-mire" was a popular game.

46–47 Take our good ... wits. trust what I say, which is five times more reliable than our five senses

49 'tis no wit it makes no sense

53 Queen Mab A fairy queen probably invented by Shakespeare.

57 atomi tiny creatures

60 joiner carpenter

60 old grub Beetle larvae that make worm holes in nuts.

62 spinners' spiders'

64 traces harness

66 film spiderweb

68–69 a round little ... maid It was believed that tiny worms would breed in the fingers of lazy maidservants.

O'er courtiers' knees, that dream on cur'sies straight,
O'er lawyers' fingers, who straight dream on fees,
O'er ladies' lips, who straight on kisses dream,
75 Which oft the angry Mab with blisters plagues,
Because their breaths with sweetmeats tainted are.
Sometime she gallops o'er a courtier's nose,
And then dreams he of smelling out a suit;
And sometime comes she with a tithe-pig's tail
80 Tickling a parson's nose as 'a lies asleep,
Then he dreams of another benefice.
Sometime she driveth o'er a soldier's neck,
And then dreams he of cutting foreign throats,
Of breaches, ambuscadoes, Spanish blades,
85 Of healths five fathom deep; and then anon
Drums in his ear, at which he starts and wakes,
And being thus frighted, swears a prayer or two,
And sleeps again. This is that very Mab
That plats the manes of horses in the night,
90 And bakes the elf-locks in foul sluttish hairs,
Which, once untangl'd, much misfortune bodes.
This is the hag, when maids lie on their backs,
That presses them and learns them first to bear,
Making them women of good carriage.
95 This is she—

ROMEO   Peace, peace, Mercutio, peace!
Thou talk'st of nothing.

MERCUTIO   True, I talk of dreams,
Which are the children of an idle brain,
Begot of nothing but vain fantasy,
Which is as thin of substance as the air,
100 And more inconstant than the wind, who woos
Even now the frozen bosom of the north,
And being anger'd puffs away from thence,
Turning his side to the dew-dropping south.

BENVOLIO This wind you talk of blows us from ourselves:
105 Supper is done, and we shall come too late.

ROMEO   I fear too early, for my mind misgives
Some consequence yet hanging in the stars
Shall bitterly begin his fearful date
With this night's revels, and expire the term
110 Of a despised life clos'd in my breast,

72 **straight** right away

76 **sweetmeats** candied fruit

78 **smelling out a suit** receiving payment for representing someone's interests at court

79 **tithe-pig** A pig offered up as a payment to the church.

81 **benefice** church appointment

84 **breaches** breaks in a line of defence

84 **ambuscadoes** ambushes

85 **healths five fathoms deep** toasts drunk with impossibly large amounts of alcohol

85 **anon** soon

90 **elf-locks** tangles

91 **much misfortune bodes** will cause more misfortune (because the elves will be angry)

93 **bear** bear the weight of a lover; bear children

94 **of good carriage** of good posture; able to carry children

101 **Even now** for a while

103 **dew-dropping** rainy

104 **from ourselves** from what we are doing

106 **misgives** fears

107 **yet hanging in the stars** that fate has in store

109 **expire the term** end

By some vile forfeit of untimely death.
But He that hath the steerage of my course
Direct my sail! On, lusty gentlemen.

BENVOLIO Strike, drum.

They march about the stage and stand to one side

Scene 5

Sunday night: CAPULET's *house. And* SERVINGMEN
come forth with napkins

FIRST SERVINGMAN   Where's Potpan, that he helps not to take away? He shift
a trencher? he scrape a trencher?

SECOND SERVINGMAN   When good manners shall lie all in one or two men's
hands, and they unwashed too, 'tis a foul thing.

5 FIRST SERVINGMAN   Away with the join-stools, remove the court-cupboard,
look to the plate. Good thou, save me a piece of
marchpane, and as thou loves me, let the porter let in
Susan Grindstone and Nell.   [*Exit* SECOND SERVINGMAN
Anthony and Potpan!

Enter two more SERVINGMEN

10 THIRD SERVINGMAN   Ay, boy, ready.

FIRST SERVINGMAN   You are looked for and called for, asked for and sought
for, in the great chamber.

FOURTH SERVINGMAN   We cannot be here and there too. Cheerly, boys, be brisk
a while, and the longer liver take all.

They retire behind

Enter CAPULET, LADY CAPULET, JULIET, TYBALT *and his*
PAGE, NURSE, *and all the* GUESTS *and* GENTLEWOMEN *to*
the Maskers

15 CAPULET   Welcome, gentlemen! Ladies that have toes
Unplagu'd with corns will walk a bout with you.
Ah, my mistresses, which of you all
Will now deny to dance? She that makes dainty,
She I'll swear hath corns. Am I come near ye now?
20 Welcome, gentlemen! I have seen the day
That I have worn a visor and could tell
A whispering tale in a fair lady's ear,
Such as would please; 'tis gone, 'tis gone, 'tis gone.

. . . .

111 forfeit payment

111 untimely premature

112–113 He that hath ... sail I'll let
God determine my life's path

1 take away clear the plates

2 trencher wooden platter

5 join-stools wooden stools

5 court-cupboard sideboard

6 look to the plate clear away the
silver

7 marchpane marzipan

7 as if

14 the longer liver take all An
expression meaning "make the most
of life."

16 walk a bout dance

18 makes dainty refuses to dance

19 Am I come near ye have I guessed
the truth

You are welcome, gentlemen. Come, musicians, play.

Music plays

25   A hall, a hall, give room! and foot it, girls.

And they dance

More light, you knaves, and turn the tables up;
And quench the fire, the room is grown too hot.
Ah, sirrah, this unlook'd-for sport comes well.
Nay, sit, nay, sit, good Cousin Capulet,
30   For you and I are past our dancing days.
How long is't now since last yourself and I
Were in a mask?

COUSIN CAPULET   Berlady, thirty years.

CAPULET   What, man, 'tis not so much, 'tis not so much:
'Tis since the nuptial of Lucentio,
35   Come Pentecost as quickly as it will,
Some five and twenty years, and then we mask'd.

COUSIN CAPULET   'Tis more, 'tis more, his son is elder, sir;
His son is thirty.

CAPULET   Will you tell me that?
His son was but a ward two years ago.

40 ROMEO   [*To a* SERVINGMAN] What lady's that which doth enrich the hand
Of yonder knight?

SERVINGMAN   I know not, sir.

ROMEO   O she doth teach the torches to burn bright!
It seems she hangs upon the cheek of night
45   As a rich jewel in an Ethiop's ear—
Beauty too rich for use, for earth too dear:
So shows a snowy dove trooping with crows,
As yonder lady o'er her fellows shows.
The measure done, I'll watch her place of stand,
50   And touching hers, make blessed my rude hand.
Did my heart love till now? forswear it, sight!
For I ne'er saw true beauty till this night.

TYBALT   This, by his voice, should be a Montague.
Fetch me my rapier, boy.   [*Exit* PAGE
                              What dares the slave
55   Come hither, cover'd with an antic face,
To fleer and scorn at our solemnity?

• •

25 A hall make way

25 foot it start dancing

28 unlook'd-for sport unexpected fun

32 Berlady by our Lady (a mild oath)

34 nuptial wedding

35 Pentecost The seventh Sunday after Easter.

38 Will you tell me that? you don't say

39 but a ward only a youth

45 Ethiop black African

46 Beauty too rich ... dear too precious for everyday life, but too valuable to be buried

47 shows looks; stands out

49 The measure done when this dance is over

50 rude rough (i.e., of lower social status)

51 forswear deny

53 should be must be

55 antic face funny mask

56 fleer make fun of

56 solemnity celebration

Now by the stock and honour of my kin,
To strike him dead I hold it not a sin.

CAPULET Why, how now, kinsman, wherefore storm you so?

60 **TYBALT** Uncle, this is a Montague, our foe:
A villain that is hither come in spite,
To scorn at our solemnity this night.

CAPULET Young Romeo is it?

TYBALT   'Tis he, that villain Romeo.

CAPULET Content thee, gentle coz, let him alone,
65 'A bears him like a portly gentleman;
And to say truth, Verona brags of him
To be a virtuous and well-govern'd youth.
I would not for the wealth of all this town
Here in my house do him disparagement;
70 Therefore be patient, take no note of him;
It is my will, the which if thou respect,
Show a fair presence, and put off these frowns,
An ill-beseeming semblance for a feast.

TYBALT It fits when such a villain is a guest:
75 I'll not endure him.

CAPULET   He shall be endur'd.
What, goodman boy, I say he shall, go to!
Am I the master here, or you? go to!
You'll not endure him? God shall mend my soul,
You'll make a mutiny among my guests!
80 You will set cock-a-hoop! you'll be the man!

TYBALT Why, uncle, 'tis a shame.

CAPULET   Go to, go to,
You are a saucy boy. Is't so indeed?
This trick may chance to scathe you, I know what.
You must contrary me! Marry, 'tis time.—
85 Well said, my hearts!—You are a princox, go,
Be quiet, or—More light, more light!—For shame,
I'll make you quiet, what!—Cheerly, my hearts!

TYBALT Patience perforce with wilful choler meeting
Makes my flesh tremble in their different greeting:
90 I will withdraw, but this intrusion shall,
Now seeming sweet, convert to bitt'rest gall.   [*Exit*

---

64 coz cousin (used for any member of an extended family)

65 portly respectable

69 do him disparagement insult him

73 ill-beseeming semblance inappropriate behaviour

76 goodman boy rude child

76 go to for shame

80 set cock-a-hoop act without restraint

83 scathe you hurt you (financially)

84 contrary me go against my wishes

85 princox insolent youth

88 perforce forced

88 choler anger

91 bitt'rest gall bitter poison

ROMEO [*To* JULIET] If I profane with my unworthiest hand
This holy shrine, the gentle sin is this,
My lips, two blushing pilgrims, ready stand
95 To smooth that rough touch with a tender kiss.

JULIET Good pilgrim, you do wrong your hand too much,
Which mannerly devotion shows in this,
For saints have hands that pilgrims' hands do touch,
And palm to palm is holy palmers' kiss.

100 ROMEO Have not saints lips, and holy palmers too?

JULIET Ay, pilgrim, lips that they must use in prayer.

ROMEO O then, dear saint, let lips do what hands do:
They pray, grant thou, lest faith turn to despair.

JULIET Saints do not move, though grant for prayers' sake.

105 ROMEO Then move not while my prayer's effect I take.
Thus from my lips, by thine, my sin is purg'd.

Kissing her

JULIET Then have my lips the sin that they have took.

ROMEO Sin from my lips? O trespass sweetly urg'd!
Give me my sin again.

Kissing her again

JULIET   You kiss by th' book.

110 NURSE Madam, your mother craves a word with you.

ROMEO What is her mother?

NURSE   Marry, bachelor,
Her mother is the lady of the house,
And a good lady, and a wise and virtuous.
I nurs'd her daughter that you talk'd withal;
115 I tell you, he that can lay hold of her
Shall have the chinks.

ROMEO   Is she a Capulet?
O dear account! my life is my foe's debt.

BENVOLIO Away, be gone, the sport is at the best.

ROMEO Ay, so I fear, the more is my unrest.

120 CAPULET Nay, gentlemen, prepare not to be gone,
We have a trifling foolish banquet towards.

They whisper in his ear

Is it e'en so? Why then I thank you all.

....

92 profane debase; defile

93 This holy shrine Romeo compares Juliet's hand to a shrine, and his own lips to pilgrims worshipping it.

97 Which mannerly … this which shows proper respect (by touching my hand)

99 holy palmers pilgrims

102 let lips do what hands do let lips touch, just as hands do

103 They pray, grant thou you should grant what lips pray for

104 Saints do not … sake. images of saints don't move, although they do grant people's prayers

105 effect result

106 purg'd removed

109 You kiss by th' book. you kiss as if you learned it in a book

116 the chinks lots of money

117 my life is my foe's debt my life is indebted to my enemy

118 the sport is at the best now is the time to get going

119 the more is my unrest that's what is making me unhappy

121 a trifling … towards a simple dessert still to come

122 Is it e'en so? is that what it is

		I thank you, honest gentlemen, good night.
		More torches here, come on! then let's to bed.
125		Ah, sirrah, by my fay, it waxes late,
		I'll to my rest. [*Exeunt all but* JULIET *and* NURSE
	JULIET	Come hither, Nurse. What is yond gentleman?
	NURSE	The son and heir of old Tiberio.
	JULIET	What's he that now is going out of door?
130	Nurse	Marry, that I think be young Petruchio.
	JULIET	What's he that follows here, that would not dance?
	NURSE	I know not.
	JULIET	Go ask his name.—If he be married,
		My grave is like to be my wedding bed.
135	NURSE	His name is Romeo, and a Montague,
		The only son of your great enemy.
	JULIET	My only love sprung from my only hate!
		Too early seen unknown, and known too late!
		Prodigious birth of love it is to me,
140		That I must love a loathed enemy.
	NURSE	What's tis? what's tis?
	JULIET	A rhyme I learnt even now
		Of one I danc'd withal.

One calls within, 'Juliet!'

	NURSE	Anon, anon!
		Come let's away, the strangers all are gone. [*Exeunt

Enter CHORUS

	CHORUS	Now old desire doth in his death-bed lie,
145		And young affection gapes to be his heir;
		That fair for which love groan'd for and would die,
		With tender Juliet match'd is now not fair.
		Now Romeo is belov'd, and loves again,
		Alike bewitched by the charm of looks;
150		But to his foe suppos'd he must complain,
		And she steal love's sweet bait from fearful hooks.
		Being held a foe, he may not have access
		To breathe such vows as lovers use to swear,
		And she as much in love, her means much less
155		To meet her new-beloved any where:
		But passion lends them power, time means, to meet,
		Temp'ring extremities with extreme sweet. [*Exit

· ·

125 by my fay by my faith

133–134 If he be … bed. if he's married, I'll die

138 Too early seen … late! I saw him before I knew who he was; and now that I do know, it's too late

139 Prodigious ill-fated; unlucky

141 even now just now

144 old desire Romeo's forgotten desire for Rosaline

145 gapes to be his heir hungers to take his place

146 That fair that fair woman (Rosaline)

148 again in return

150 complain declare his love

151 fearful dangerous

152 held considered

157 Temp'ring extremities making hardships easier to bear

ACT 2 Scene 1

Late Sunday night: outside CAPULET's *orchard. Enter*
ROMEO *alone*

ROMEO   Can I go forward when my heart is here?
Turn back, dull earth, and find thy centre out.

ROMEO *withdraws*

Enter BENVOLIO *with* MERCUTIO

BENVOLIO   Romeo! my cousin Romeo! Romeo!

MERCUTIO   He is wise,
And on my life hath stol'n him home to bed.

5   BENVOLIO   He ran this way and leapt this orchard wall.
Call, good Mercutio.

MERCUTIO   Nay, I'll conjure too.
Romeo! humours! madman! passion! lover!
Appear thou in the likeness of a sigh,
Speak but one rhyme, and I am satisfied;
10   Cry but 'Ay me!', pronounce but 'love' and 'dove',
Speak to my gossip Venus one fair word,
One nickname for her purblind son and heir,
Young Abraham Cupid, he that shot so trim
When King Cophetua lov'd the beggar-maid.
15   He heareth not, he stirreth not, he moveth not,
The ape is dead, and I must conjure him.
I conjure thee by Rosaline's bright eyes,
By her high forehead and her scarlet lip,
By her fine foot, straight leg, and quivering thigh,
20   And the demesnes that there adjacent lie,
That in thy likeness thou appear to us.

BENVOLIO   And if he hear thee, thou wilt anger him.

MERCUTIO   This cannot anger him; 'twould anger him
To raise a spirit in his mistress' circle,
25   Of some strange nature, letting it there stand
Till she had laid it and conjur'd it down:
That were some spite. My invocation
Is fair and honest: in his mistress' name
I conjure only but to raise up him.

30   BENVOLIO   Come, he hath hid himself among these trees
To be consorted with the humorous night:

. . . .

2 dull earth i.e., Romeo

7 humours obsessions

11 my gossip my buddy

11 Venus Roman goddess of love.

12 purblind totally blind

13 Abraham patriarch; old man

13 trim accurately

14 King Cophetua A legendary king who fell in love and married a beggar-maid.

16 The ape is dead Romeo isn't responding.

20 demesnes domains; regions

21 in thy likeness as yourself

24 raise a spirit ... circle conjure up a ghost; have sexual intercourse

26 laid satisfied

26 conjur'd it down sent it back to the spirit world

27 That were some spite Romeo would have reason to be angry then

31 To be consorted with to keep company with

31 humorous gloomy; moody

	Blind is his love, and best befits the dark.
MERCUTIO	If love be blind, love cannot hit the mark.
	Now will he sit under a medlar tree,
35	And wish his mistress were that kind of fruit
	As maids call medlars, when they laugh alone.
	O Romeo, that she were, O that she were
	An open-arse, thou a pop'rin pear!
	Romeo, good night, I'll to my truckle-bed,
40	This field-bed is too cold for me to sleep.
	Come, shall we go?
BENVOLIO	Go then, for 'tis in vain
	To seek him here that means not to be found.

                                        [*Exit with* MERCUTIO

Scene 2

Very late Sunday night/early Monday morning:
CAPULET's *orchard.* ROMEO *advances*

ROMEO	He jests at scars that never felt a wound.
	But soft, what light through yonder window breaks?
	It is the east, and Juliet is the sun.
	Arise, fair sun, and kill the envious moon,
5	Who is already sick and pale with grief
	That thou, her maid, art far more fair than she.
	Be not her maid, since she is envious;
	Her vestal livery is but sick and green,
	And none but fools do wear it; cast it off.

JULIET *appears aloft as at a window*

10	It is my lady, O it is my love:
	O that she knew she were!
	She speaks, yet she says nothing; what of that?
	Her eye discourses, I will answer it.
	I am too bold, 'tis not to me she speaks:
15	Two of the fairest stars in all the heaven,
	Having some business, do entreat her eyes,
	To twinkle in their spheres till they return.
	What if her eyes were there, they in her head?
	The brightness of her cheek would shame those stars,
20	As daylight doth a lamp; her eyes in heaven
	Would through the airy region stream so bright

- -

34 medlar tree A kind of tree with fruit similar to small apples.

38 pop'rin pear A type of pear; also a slang term for a penis.

39 truckle-bed A small bed that could be stored under a larger bed.

2 But soft but wait

8 vestal livery Clothes worn by the vestal virgins, priestesses of the moon goddess Diana.

8 sick and green Young girls were prone to "greensickness" (anemia)

9 none but fools do wear it Romeo is comparing the suit worn by followers of Diana (i.e., virgins) to the green-and-yellow uniform of a clown.

13 Her eye discourses her eyes speak volumes

17 in their spheres in their orbit

That birds would sing and think it were not night.
See how she leans her cheek upon her hand!
O that I were a glove upon that hand,
25   That I might touch that cheek!

JULIET   Ay me!

ROMEO   [*Aside*]   She speaks.
O speak again, bright angel, for thou art
As glorious to this night, being o'er my head,
As is a winged messenger of heaven
Unto the white-upturned wond'ring eyes
30   Of mortals that fall back to gaze on him,
When he bestrides the lazy puffing clouds,
And sails upon the bosom of the air.

JULIET   O Romeo, Romeo, wherefore art thou Romeo?
Deny thy father and refuse thy name;
35   Or if thou wilt not, be but sworn my love,
And I'll no longer be a Capulet.

ROMEO   [*Aside*] Shall I hear more, or shall I speak at this?

JULIET   'Tis but thy name that is my enemy;
Thou art thyself, though not a Montague.
40   What's Montague? It is nor hand nor foot,
Nor arm nor face, nor any other part
Belonging to a man. O be some other name!
What's in a name? That which we call a rose
By any other word would smell as sweet;
45   So Romeo would, were he not Romeo call'd,
Retain that dear perfection which he owes
Without that title. Romeo, doff thy name,
And for thy name, which is no part of thee,
Take all myself.

ROMEO   I take thee at thy word:
50   Call me but love, and I'll be new baptis'd;
Henceforth I never will be Romeo.

JULIET   What man art thou that thus bescreen'd in night
So stumblest on my counsel?

ROMEO   By a name
I know not how to tell thee who I am.
55   My name, dear saint, is hateful to myself,
Because it is an enemy to thee;
Had I it written, I would tear the word.

. . . .

28 winged messenger angel

31 bestrides straddles

33 wherefore why

34 Deny thy father ... name forget your family and reject your own name (i.e., Montague)

39 Thou art thyself ... Montague you would still be yourself if you weren't called Montague

46 owes owns

47 doff throw off

48 for thy name in exchange for giving up your name.

50 Call me but love just call me your love

52 bescreen'd hidden

53 counsel private conversation

	JULIET	My ears have yet not drunk a hundred words
		Of thy tongue's uttering, yet I know the sound.
60		Art thou not Romeo, and a Montague?
	ROMEO	Neither, fair maid, if either thee dislike.
	JULIET	How cam'st thou hither, tell me, and wherefore?
		The orchard walls are high and hard to climb,
		And the place death, considering who thou art,
65		If any of my kinsmen find thee here.
	ROMEO	With love's light wings did I o'erperch these walls,
		For stony limits cannot hold love out,
		And what love can do, that dares love attempt:
		Therefore thy kinsmen are no stop to me.
70	JULIET	If they do see thee, they will murder thee.
	ROMEO	Alack, there lies more peril in thine eye
		Than twenty of their swords. Look thou but sweet,
		And I am proof against their enmity.
	JULIET	I would not for the world they saw thee here.
75	ROMEO	I have night's cloak to hide me from their eyes,
		And but thou love me, let them find me here;
		My life were better ended by their hate,
		Than death prorogued, wanting of thy love.
	JULIET	By whose direction found'st thou out this place?
80	ROMEO	By Love, that first did prompt me to enquire:
		He lent me counsel, and I lent him eyes.
		I am no pilot, yet wert thou as far
		As that vast shore wash'd with the farthest sea,
		I should adventure for such merchandise.
85	JULIET	Thou knowest the mask of night is on my face,
		Else would a maiden blush bepaint my cheek
		For that which thou hast heard me speak tonight.
		Fain would I dwell on form, fain, fain deny
		What I have spoke, but farewell compliment.
90		Dost thou love me? I know thou wilt say 'Ay';
		And I will take thy word; yet if thou swear'st,
		Thou mayst prove false: at lovers' perjuries
		They say Jove laughs. O gentle Romeo,
		If thou dost love, pronounce it faithfully;
95		Or if thou think'st I am too quickly won,
		I'll frown and be perverse, and say thee nay,
		So thou wilt woo, but else not for the world.

. . . .

58 My ears have yet not drunk I haven't even heard you speak

61 if either thee dislike if you don't like either of them

62 How cam'st thou hither how did you get here

66 o'erperch fly over

72 Look thou but sweet look at me kindly

73 I am proof against their enmity they can never hurt me (proof: protected)

76 but unless

77–78 My life were … prorogued I'd rather they killed me now, than put off death to a later date

84 I should adventure for such merchandise I would dare to travel that far to find you

88 Fain would I dwell on form I would happily observe the rules of politeness and proper behaviour

89 but farewell compliment but forget about such formalities

92 perjuries broken vows

93 Jove Jupiter, the Roman god of oath-taking, thunder, and the sky.

96 perverse difficult

96 say thee nay refuse you

97 So thou wilt woo if you will keep chasing me

In truth, fair Montague, I am too fond,
And therefore thou mayst think my behaviour light:
100 But trust me, gentleman, I'll prove more true
Than those that have more coying to be strange.
I should have been more strange, I must confess,
But that thou overheard'st, ere I was ware,
My true-love passion; therefore pardon me,
105 And not impute this yielding to light love,
Which the dark night hath so discovered.

ROMEO Lady, by yonder blessed moon I vow,
That tips with silver all these fruit-tree tops—

JULIET O swear not by the moon, th'inconstant moon,
110 That monthly changes in her circl'd orb,
Lest that thy love prove likewise variable.

ROMEO What shall I swear by?

JULIET   Do not swear at all;
Or if thou wilt, swear by thy gracious self,
Which is the god of my idolatry,
115 And I'll believe thee.

ROMEO   If my heart's dear love—

JULIET Well, do not swear. Although I joy in thee,
I have no joy of this contract tonight,
It is too rash, too unadvis'd, too sudden,
Too like the lightning, which doth cease to be
120 Ere one can say 'It lightens'. Sweet, good night:
This bud of love, by summer's ripening breath,
May prove a beauteous flower when next we meet.
Good night, good night! as sweet repose and rest
Come to thy heart as that within my breast.

125 **ROMEO** O wilt thou leave me so unsatisfied?

JULIET What satisfaction canst thou have tonight?

ROMEO Th'exchange of thy love's faithful vow for mine.

JULIET I gave thee mine before thou didst request it;
And yet I would it were to give again.

130 **ROMEO** Wouldst thou withdraw it? for what purpose, love?

JULIET But to be frank and give it thee again,
And yet I wish but for the thing I have:
My bounty is as boundless as the sea,
My love as deep; the more I give to thee
135 The more I have, for both are infinite.

98 too fond too infatuated
99 light too forward
101 those that have … strange those that are better at playing it cool
102 strange distant
103 ere I was ware before I knew you were there
105 impute attribute
105 light love shallow feelings
106 discovered revealed
109 inconstant changeable
110 circl'd orb round sphere
111 Lest that thy … variable or your love may turn out to be just as changeable as the moon
114 the god of my idolatry the god I worship
131 frank generous
132 but only

NURSE *calls within*

I hear some noise within; dear love, adieu!—
Anon, good Nurse!—Sweet Montague, be true.
Stay but a little, I will come again.   [*Exit above*

ROMEO O blessed, blessed night! I am afeard,
140   Being in night, all this is but a dream,
         Too flattering-sweet to be substantial.

Enter JULIET *above*

JULIET Three words, dear Romeo, and good night indeed.
         If that thy bent of love be honourable,
         Thy purpose marriage, send me word tomorrow,
145   By one that I'll procure to come to thee,
         Where and what time thou wilt perform the rite,
         And all my fortunes at thy foot I'll lay,
         And follow thee my lord throughout the world.

NURSE   [*Within*] Madam!

150 JULIET I come, anon.—But if thou meanest not well,
         I do beseech thee—

NURSE   [*Within*]   Madam!

JULIET   By and by I come—
         To cease thy strife, and leave me to my grief.
         Tomorrow will I send.

ROMEO   So thrive my soul—

JULIET   A thousand times good night!   [*Exit above*

155 ROMEO A thousand times the worse, to want thy light.
         Love goes toward love as schoolboys from their books,
         But love from love, toward school with heavy looks.

Retiring slowly

Enter JULIET *again above*

JULIET Hist, Romeo, hist! O for a falc'ner's voice,
         To lure this tassel-gentle back again:
160   Bondage is hoarse, and may not speak aloud,
         Else would I tear the cave where Echo lies,
         And make her airy tongue more hoarse than mine
         With repetition of my Romeo's name.

ROMEO   It is my soul that calls upon my name.
165   How silver-sweet sound lovers' tongues by night,

. . . .

137 Anon I'm coming

138 Stay wait

141 Too flattering … substantial too delightful to be real

143 bent purpose; intention

145 procure get

152 cease thy strife stop trying (to woo me)

158–159 O for … again if only I could call him back as a falconer recalls his hawk

160 Bondage is hoarse Juliet compares herself to a prisoner who has been silenced.

161 Else would I … lies Echo was a nymph who cried because her love for Narcissus was not returned.

Like softest music to attending ears!

JULIET   Romeo!

ROMEO   My niësse?

JULIET   What a'clock tomorrow
Shall I send to thee?

ROMEO   By the hour of nine.

JULIET   I will not fail, 'tis twenty year till then.
170   I have forgot why I did call thee back.

ROMEO   Let me stand here till thou remember it.

JULIET   I shall forget, to have thee still stand there,
Rememb'ring how I love thy company.

ROMEO   And I'll still stay, to have thee still forget,
175   Forgetting any other home but this.

JULIET   'Tis almost morning, I would have thee gone:
And yet no farther than a wanton's bird,
That lets it hop a little from his hand,
Like a poor prisoner in his twisted gyves,
180   And with a silken thread plucks it back again,
So loving-jealous of his liberty.

ROMEO   I would I were thy bird.

JULIET   Sweet, so would I,
Yet I should kill thee with much cherishing.
Good night, good night! Parting is such sweet sorrow,
185   That I shall say good night till it be morrow.   [*Exit above*

ROMEO   Sleep dwell upon thine eyes, peace in thy breast!
Would I were sleep and peace, so sweet to rest!
Hence will I to my ghostly sire's close cell,
His help to crave, and my dear hap to tell.   [*Exit*

Scene 3

Monday morning: FRIAR LAWRENCE's *cell. Enter* FRIAR
LAWRENCE *alone, with a basket*

FRIAR LAWRENCE   The grey-ey'd morn smiles on the frowning night,
Check'ring the eastern clouds with streaks of light;
And fleckled darkness like a drunkard reels
From forth day's path and Titan's fiery wheels:
5   Now ere the sun advance his burning eye,
The day to cheer, and night's dank dew to dry,
I must upfill this osier cage of ours

----

167 niësse A fledgling hawk.

177 wanton's bird A spoiled child's pet bird, kept on a leash.

179 gyves leg-irons

188 my ghostly sire's close cell my holy father's private quarters (Romeo is referring to Friar Lawrence)

189 crave beg

189 dear hap great luck

3–4 fleckled darkness … wheels red-streaked night staggers like a drunkard out of the way of daylight and the sun

7 osier cage wicker basket

With baleful weeds and precious-juiced flowers.
The earth that's nature's mother is her tomb;
10 What is her burying grave, that is her womb;
And from her womb children of divers kind
We sucking on her natural bosom find:
Many for many virtues excellent,
None but for some, and yet all different.
15 O mickle is the powerful grace that lies
In plants, herbs, stones, and their true qualities:
For nought so vile, that on the earth doth live,
But to the earth some special good doth give;
Nor ought so good but, strain'd from that fair use,
20 Revolts from true birth, stumbling on abuse.
Virtue itself turns vice, being misapplied,
And vice sometime by action dignified.

Enter ROMEO

Within the infant rind of this weak flower
Poison hath residence, and medicine power:
25 For this, being smelt, with that part cheers each part,
Being tasted, stays all senses with the heart.
Two such opposed kings encamp them still
In man as well as herbs, grace and rude will;
And where the worser is predominant,
30 Full soon the canker death eats up that plant.

ROMEO Good morrow, father.

FRIAR LAWRENCE   Benedicite!
What early tongue so sweet saluteth me?
Young son, it argues a distemper'd head
So soon to bid good morrow to thy bed:
35 Care keeps his watch in every old man's eye,
And where care lodges, sleep will never lie;
But where unbruised youth with unstuff'd brain
Doth couch his limbs, there golden sleep doth reign.
Therefore thy earliness doth me assure
40 Thou art uprous'd with some distemp'rature;
Or if not so, then here I hit it right,
Our Romeo hath not been in bed tonight.

ROMEO That last is true, the sweeter rest was mine.

FRIAR LAWRENCE God pardon sin! wast thou with Rosaline?

. . . .

8 baleful poisonous

11 divers many

13–14 Many for many … different
many plants have more than one use,
all of them have at least a few good
properties, and yet all are different

15 mickle mighty

17–18 nought so … give even the
vilest living thing has some good
qualities

19–20 Nor ought so … abuse nor is
anything so good that it can't be used
inappropriately to cause harm

23 infant immature

25 being smelt … part when we
smell it, its scent ("that part") warms
up every part of our body

**26 stays all senses with the
heart** kills all the senses by making
the heart stop beating

27 encamp them still establish
themselves

28 grace and rude will virtue and vice

30 canker canker-worm (a pest that
eats a plant from the inside)

33–34 it argues a … bed you must
be upset to be up so early

40 uprous'd with some distemp'rature
awakened by a troubled mind

45 ROMEO   With Rosaline, my ghostly father? no;
          I have forgot that name, and that name's woe.

   FRIAR LAWRENCE   That's my good son, but where hast thou been then?

   ROMEO   I'll tell thee ere thou ask it me again:
          I have been feasting with mine enemy,
50   Where on a sudden one hath wounded me
          That's by me wounded; both our remedies
          Within thy help and holy physic lies.
          I bear no hatred, blessed man; for lo,
          My intercession likewise steads my foe.

55 FRIAR LAWRENCE   Be plain, good son, and homely in thy drift,
          Riddling confession finds but riddling shrift.

   ROMEO   Then plainly know, my heart's dear love is set
          On the fair daughter of rich Capulet;
          As mine on hers, so hers is set on mine,
60   And all combin'd, save what thou must combine
          By holy marriage. When and where and how
          We met, we woo'd, and made exchange of vow,
          I'll tell thee as we pass, but this I pray,
          That thou consent to marry us today.

65 FRIAR LAWRENCE   Holy Saint Francis, what a change is here!
          Is Rosaline, that thou didst love so dear,
          So soon forsaken? Young men's love then lies
          Not truly in their hearts, but in their eyes.
          Jesu Maria, what a deal of brine
70   Hath wash'd thy sallow cheeks for Rosaline!
          How much salt water thrown away in waste,
          To season love, that of it doth not taste!
          The sun not yet thy sighs from heaven clears,
          Thy old groans yet ringing in mine ancient ears;
75   Lo here upon thy cheek the stain doth sit
          Of an old tear that is not wash'd off yet.
          If e'er thou wast thyself, and these woes thine,
          Thou and these woes were all for Rosaline.
          And art thou chang'd? Pronounce this sentence then:
80   Women may fall, when there's no strength in men.

   ROMEO   Thou chid'st me oft for loving Rosaline.

   FRIAR LAWRENCE   For doting, not for loving, pupil mine.

   ROMEO   And bad'st me bury love.

   FRIAR LAWRENCE   Not in a grave,
          To lay one in, another out to have.

---

45 ghostly spiritual

50–51 on a sudden ... wounded I've been wounded by an enemy, who has also been wounded by me

52 holy physic spiritual medicine

54 intercession request

54 steads helps

55 homely in thy drift direct in saying what you mean

56 shrift absolution from your sins

69 brine salt water (i.e., tears)

77 If e'er thou wast thyself if you were sincere

80 Women may fall it's understandable if women fall into sin

81 chid'st scolded

82 doting shallow infatuation

83 bad'st bade; ordered

85	ROMEO	I pray thee chide me not. Her I love now
		Doth grace for grace and love for love allow;
		The other did not so.
	FRIAR LAWRENCE	O she knew well
		Thy love did read by rote, that could not spell.
		But come, young waverer, come go with me,
90		In one respect I'll thy assistant be:
		For this alliance may so happy prove
		To turn your households' rancour to pure love.
	ROMEO	O let us hence, I stand on sudden haste.
	FRIAR LAWRENCE	Wisely and slow, they stumble that run fast. [*Exeunt*

Scene 4

Verona: a street. Enter BENVOLIO *and* MERCUTIO

	MERCUTIO	Where the dev'l should this Romeo be?
		Came he not home tonight?
	BENVOLIO	Not to his father's, I spoke with his man.
	MERCUTIO	Why, that same pale hard-hearted wench, that Rosaline,
5		Torments him so, that he will sure run mad.
	BENVOLIO	Tybalt, the kinsman to old Capulet,
		Hath sent a letter to his father's house.
	MERCUTIO	A challenge, on my life.
	BENVOLIO	Romeo will answer it.
10	MERCUTIO	Any man that can write may answer a letter.
	BENVOLIO	Nay, he will answer the letter's master, how he dares,
		being dared.
	MERCUTIO	Alas, poor Romeo, he is already dead, stabbed with a
		white wench's black eye, run through the ear with a
15		love-song, the very pin of his heart cleft with the blind
		bow-boy's butt-shaft; and is he a man to encounter
		Tybalt?
	BENVOLIO	Why, what is Tybalt?
	MERCUTIO	More than Prince of Cats. O, he's the courageous
20		captain of compliments: he fights as you sing prick-
		song, keeps time, distance, and proportion; he rests his
		minim rests, one, two, and the third in your bosom; the
		very butcher of a silk button, a duellist, a duellist; a
		gentleman of the very first house, of the first and second

86 Doth grace for … allow returns my love, and favours me as much as I do her

88 Thy love did … spell your love wasn't true (it did not actually read the words it spoke, but had merely learned them by heart)

92 rancour hatred

93 stand on sudden haste insist on going quickly

8 challenge Tybalt is challenging Romeo to a fight.

15–16 the very pin … butt-shaft the bull's eye of his heart pierced by Cupid's thick arrow

19 Prince of Cats A character in a well-known fable, whose name was Tibert or Tibault.

20 captain of compliments champion of the latest Italian style of swordplay

20–21 prick-song sheet music

21–22 he rests his minim rests he pauses briefly between strokes (minim: a very short musical note)

22–23 the very butcher of a silk button he can slice the buttons right off your jacket

23–24 a gentleman of the very first house a top-notch duelist

25   cause. Ah, the immortal 'passado', the 'punto reverso', the 'hay'!

BENVOLIO The what?

MERCUTIO The pox of such antic, lisping, affecting phantasimes,
these new tuners of accent! 'By Jesu, a very good blade!
30   a very tall man! a very good whore!' Why, is not this a
lamentable thing, grandsire, that we should be thus
afflicted with these strange flies, these fashion-mongers,
these pardon-me's, who stand so much on the new
form, that they cannot sit at ease on the old bench? O
35   their bones, their bones!

Enter ROMEO

BENVOLIO Here comes Romeo, here comes Romeo.

MERCUTIO Without his roe, like a dried herring: O flesh, flesh, how
art thou fishified! Now is he for the numbers that
Petrarch flowed in. Laura to his lady was a kitchen
40   wench (marry, she had a better love to berhyme her),
Dido a dowdy, Cleopatra a gipsy, Helen and Hero
hildings and harlots, Thisbe a grey eye or so, but not to
the purpose. Signior Romeo, 'bon jour'! there's a French
salutation to your French slop. You gave us the
45   counterfeit fairly last night.

ROMEO Good morrow to you both. What counterfeit did I give
you?

MERCUTIO The slip, sir, the slip, can you not conceive?

ROMEO Pardon, good Mercutio, my business was great, and in
50   such a case as mine a man may strain courtesy.

MERCUTIO That's as much as to say, such a case as yours constrains
a man to bow in the hams.

ROMEO Meaning to cur'sy.

MERCUTIO Thou hast most kindly hit it.

55 **ROMEO** A most courteous exposition.

MERCUTIO Nay, I am the very pink of courtesy.

ROMEO Pink for flower.

MERCUTIO Right.

ROMEO Why then is my pump well flowered.

60 **MERCUTIO** Sure wit! Follow me this jest now, till thou hast worn
out thy pump, that when the single sole of it is worn, the
jest may remain, after the wearing, solely singular.

24–25 first and second cause reasons for challenging someone to a duel

25 'passado' … 'hay' fencing moves

28–29 The pox … accent! a plague on such silly, affected posers, with their fancy ways of talking

33–34 who stand so … bench who are so caught up in the new trends, they are no longer at ease with the old ways

38–39 Now is he … in. now he likes the type of poem that Petrarch wrote

41 Dido Queen of Carthage. Each of the examples Mercutio gives here involves a tragic love affair.

41 dowdy unattractive woman

42 hildings and harlots loose women and prostitutes

44 French slop baggy trousers

44–45 gave us the counterfeit played a trick on us

51–52 constrains a man … hams makes a man weak in the legs

56 pink best example; flower

59 pump shoe

61 single thin

62 solely singular remarkable

	ROMEO	O single-soled jest, solely singular for the singleness!
	MERCUTIO	Come between us, good Benvolio, my wits faints.
65	ROMEO	Swits and spurs, swits and spurs, or I'll cry a match.
	MERCUTIO	Nay, if our wits run the wild-goose chase, I am done; for thou hast more of the wild goose in one of thy wits than, I am sure, I have in my whole five. Was I with you there for the goose?
70	ROMEO	Thou wast never with me for any thing when thou wast not there for the goose.
	MERCUTIO	I will bite thee by the ear for that jest.
	ROMEO	Nay, good goose, bite not.
	MERCUTIO	Thy wit is very bitter sweeting, it is a most sharp sauce.
75	ROMEO	And is it not then well served in to a sweet goose?
	MERCUTIO	O here's a wit of cheverel, that stretches from an inch narrow to an ell broad!
	ROMEO	I stretch it out for that word 'broad', which, added to the goose, proves thee far and wide a broad goose.
80	MERCUTIO	Why, is not this better now than groaning for love? Now art thou sociable, now art thou Romeo; now art thou what thou art, by art as well as by nature, for this drivelling love is like a great natural that runs lolling up and down to hide his bauble in a hole.
85	BENVOLIO	Stop there, stop there.
	MERCUTIO	Thou desirest me to stop in my tale against the hair.
	BENVOLIO	Thou wouldst else have made thy tale large.
90	MERCUTIO	O thou art deceived; I would have made it short, for I was come to the whole depth of my tale, and meant indeed to occupy the argument no longer.
	ROMEO	Here's goodly gear!

Enter NURSE *and her man* PETER

		A sail, a sail!
	MERCUTIO	Two, two: a shirt and a smock.
	NURSE	Peter!
95	PETER	Anon.
	NURSE	My fan, Peter.
	MERCUTIO	Good Peter, to hide her face, for her fan's the fairer face.
	NURSE	God ye good morrow, gentlemen.

---

63 O, single-soled … singleness! O silly joke

65 Swits and spurs keep pushing yourself to be witty (swits: whips)

65 cry a match declare myself the winner

67 wild goose dimwit

68 five five senses

68–69 Was I … goose? did I get a point off you with that "goose" joke

71 goose prostitute; fool

76 cheverel Soft, stretchy leather.

77 ell A unit of measure (about 115 cm).

79 broad goose A goose that does not lay its own eggs.

82 by art by skill

83 natural idiot

84 hide his bauble in a hole hide his jester's stick in a hole (with a sexual double meaning)

86 stop in my tale stop telling my story (also a sexual joke)

86 against the hair against my will

91 gear trash

92 A sail, a sail! Romeo compares the Nurse's clothing to a ship's sail.

MERCUTIO God ye good den, fair gentlewoman.

100 NURSE Is it good den?

MERCUTIO 'Tis no less, I tell ye, for the bawdy hand of the dial is
now upon the prick of noon.

NURSE Out upon you, what a man are you?

ROMEO One, gentlewoman, that God hath made, himself to
105 mar.

NURSE By my troth, it is well said: 'for himself to mar', quoth'a?
Gentlemen, can any of you tell me where I may find the
young Romeo?

ROMEO I can tell you, but young Romeo will be older when you
110 have found him than he was when you sought him: I
am the youngest of that name, for fault of a worse.

NURSE You say well.

MERCUTIO Yea, is the worst well? Very well took, i'faith, wisely,
wisely.

115 NURSE If you be he, sir, I desire some confidence with you.

BENVOLIO She will indite him to some supper.

MERCUTIO A bawd, a bawd, a bawd! So ho!

ROMEO What hast thou found?

MERCUTIO No hare, sir, unless a hare, sir, in a lenten pie, that is
120 something stale and hoar ere it be spent.

He walks by them and sings

An old hare hoar,
And an old hare hoar,
Is very good meat in Lent;
But a hare that is hoar
125 Is too much for a score,
When it hoars ere it be spent.

Romeo, will you come to your father's? We'll to dinner
thither.

ROMEO I will follow you.

130 MERCUTIO Farewell, ancient lady, farewell, lady, [*Singing*] 'lady,
lady'.   [*Exeunt* MERCUTIO *and* BENVOLIO

NURSE I pray you, sir, what saucy merchant was this that was so
full of his ropery?

ROMEO A gentleman, Nurse, that loves to hear himself talk, and
135 will speak more in a minute than he will stand to in a
month.

99 God ye good den good evening

101 dial clock face; woman

102 prick point; penis

106 quoth'a he said

111 fault want

115 confidence The Nurse means to
say "conference."

116 indite Benvolio mispronounces
"invite" on purpose.

117 bawd brothel keeper; hare

117 So ho! tally ho (a hunting cry)

119 lenten pie pie eaten during
Lent (when people ate very little
meat)

120 hoar mouldy (a pun on
"whore")

125 score bill

133 ropery bawdy jokes

135 stand to abide by; be true to

NURSE	And 'a speak any thing against me, I'll take him down, and 'a were lustier than he is, and twenty such Jacks; and if I cannot, I'll find those that shall. Scurvy knave, I am none of his flirt-gills, I am none of his skains-mates. [*She turns to* PETER, *her man*] And thou must stand by too and suffer every knave to use me at his pleasure!
PETER	I saw no man use you at his pleasure; if I had, my weapon should quickly have been out. I warrant you, I dare draw as soon as another man, if I see occasion in a good quarrel, and the law on my side.
NURSE	Now afore God, I am so vexed that every part about me quivers. Scurvy knave! Pray you, sir, a word: and as I told you, my young lady bid me enquire you out; what she bid me say, I will keep to myself. But first let me tell ye, if ye should lead her in a fool's paradise, as they say, it were a very gross kind of behaviour, as they say; for the gentlewoman is young; and therefore, if you should deal double with her, truly it were an ill thing to be offered to any gentlewoman, and very weak dealing.
ROMEO	Nurse, commend me to thy lady and mistress. I protest unto thee—
NURSE	Good heart, and i'faith I will tell her as much. Lord, Lord, she will be a joyful woman.
ROMEO	What wilt thou tell her, Nurse? thou dost not mark me.
NURSE	I will tell her, sir, that you do protest, which, as I take it, is a gentleman-like offer.
ROMEO	Bid her devise Some means to come to shrift this afternoon, And there she shall at Friar Lawrence' cell Be shriv'd and married. Here is for thy pains.
NURSE	No truly, sir, not a penny.
ROMEO	Go to, I say you shall.
NURSE	This afternoon, sir? Well, she shall be there.
ROMEO	And stay, good Nurse, behind the abbey wall: Within this hour my man shall be with thee, And bring thee cords made like a tackl'd stair, Which to the high top-gallant of my joy Must be my convoy in the secret night. Farewell, be trusty, and I'll quit thy pains. Farewell, commend me to thy mistress.

Line numbers: 140, 145, 150, 155, 160, 165, 170, 175

· ·

138 Jacks rogues; rascals

140 flirt-gills flirty women

140 skains-mates gang members

144 weapon sword; penis

154 deal double mislead

155 weak dealing low behaviour

156 protest swear; promise

160 thou dost not mark me you don't understand what I'm saying

164 shrift confession

166 shriv'd have her sins forgiven in the sacrament of reconciliation

166 for thy pains something for your trouble (Romeo hands the Nurse some money)

172 tackl'd stair rope ladder

173 top-gallant highest sail on a ship

174 convoy means of transport

175 quit thy pains repay your efforts

NURSE	Now God in heaven bless thee! Hark you, sir.
ROMEO	What say'st thou, my dear Nurse?
NURSE	Is your man secret? Did you ne'er hear say,

180   'Two may keep counsel, putting one away'?

ROMEO   'Warrant thee, my man's as true as steel.

NURSE   Well, sir, my mistress is the sweetest lady—Lord, Lord!
when 'twas a little prating thing—O, there is a
nobleman in town, one Paris, that would fain lay knife

185   aboard; but she, good soul, had as lieve see a toad, a very
toad, as see him. I anger her sometimes, and tell her that
Paris is the properer man, but I'll warrant you, when I
say so, she looks as pale as any clout in the versal world.
Doth not rosemary and Romeo begin both with

190   a letter?

ROMEO   Ay, Nurse, what of that? Both with an R.

NURSE   Ah, mocker, that's the dog-name. R is for the—no, I
know it begins with some other letter—and she hath
the prettiest sententious of it, of you and rosemary, that

195   it would do you good to hear it.

ROMEO   Commend me to thy lady.

NURSE   Ay, a thousand times.   [*Exit* ROMEO
                            Peter!

PETER   Anon.

NURSE   [*Handing him her fan*] Before and apace.   [*Exit after* PETER

Scene 5

CAPULET's *house: enter* JULIET

JULIET   The clock struck nine when I did send the Nurse;
In half an hour she promis'd to return.
Perchance she cannot meet him: that's not so.
O, she is lame! Love's heralds should be thoughts,

5   Which ten times faster glides than the sun's beams,
Driving back shadows over low'ring hills;
Therefore do nimble-pinion'd doves draw Love,
And therefore hath the wind-swift Cupid wings.
Now is the sun upon the highmost hill

10   Of this day's journey, and from nine till twelve
Is three long hours, yet she is not come.
Had she affections and warm youthful blood,

---

179 secret reliable; trustworthy

180 keep counsel keep a secret

181 'Warrant thee I swear

183 prating babbling

184–185 would fain lay knife aboard
would like to claim her (Juliet) as his

185 had as lieve would prefer to

187 properer better looking

188 clout dishrag

188 in the versal world in the whole
wide world (versal: universal)

194 sententious The Nurse means
to say "sentence," meaning proverb.

192–193 R is for ... letter The word
the Nurse is about to say is probably
"arse." (Like many servants at the
time, she is unable to read or write.)

3 Perchance perhaps

6 low'ring frowning; menacing

7 Therefore do ... Love that's why
Venus, the goddess of love, has
fast-flying doves to draw her carriage
across the sky

12 affections feelings

She would be as swift in motion as a ball;
My words would bandy her to my sweet love,
15 And his to me.
But old folks, many feign as they were dead,
Unwieldy, slow, heavy, and pale as lead.

Enter NURSE *with* PETER

O God, she comes! O honey Nurse, what news?
Hast thou met with him? Send thy man away.

20 NURSE Peter, stay at the gate. [*Exit* PETER

JULIET Now, good sweet Nurse—O Lord, why look'st thou sad?
Though news be sad, yet tell them merrily;
If good, thou shamest the music of sweet news
By playing it to me with so sour a face.

25 NURSE I am a-weary, give me leave a while.
Fie, how my bones ache! What a jaunce have I!

JULIET I would thou hadst my bones, and I thy news.
Nay, come, I pray thee speak, good, good Nurse, speak.

NURSE Jesu, what haste! can you not stay a while?
30 Do you not see that I am out of breath?

JULIET How art thou out of breath, when thou hast breath
To say to me that thou art out of breath?
The excuse that thou dost make in this delay
Is longer than the tale thou dost excuse.
35 Is thy news good or bad? Answer to that.
Say either, and I'll stay the circumstance:
Let me be satisfied, is't good or bad?

NURSE Well, you have made a simple choice, you know not how
to choose a man: Romeo? no, not he; though his face be
40 better than any man's, yet his leg excels all men's, and for
a hand and a foot and a body, though they be not to be
talked on, yet they are past compare. He is not the
flower of courtesy, but I'll warrant him, as gentle as a
lamb. Go thy ways, wench, serve God. What, have you
45 dined at home?

JULIET No, no! But all this did I know before.
What says he of our marriage, what of that?

NURSE Lord, how my head aches! what a head have I!
It beats as it would fall in twenty pieces.
50 My back a't'other side—ah, my back, my back!

. . . .

14 bandy volley (as in tennis)

16 feign as they were dead act like
they're dead

26 jaunce tiring, rough journey

29 stay wait

33 in for

36 stay the circumstance wait for
the rest

38 simple foolish

43 flower of courtesy most polite

50 a't' on the

Beshrew your heart for sending me about
To catch my death with jauncing up and down!

JULIET   I'faith, I am sorry that thou art not well.
Sweet, sweet, sweet Nurse, tell me, what says my love?

55 NURSE   Your love says, like an honest gentleman,
And a courteous, and a kind, and a handsome,
And I warrant a virtuous—Where is your mother?

JULIET   Where is my mother? why, she is within,
Where should she be? How oddly thou repliest:
60   'Your love says, like an honest gentleman,
"Where is your mother?"'

NURSE   O God's lady dear,
Are you so hot? Marry come up, I trow;
Is this the poultice for my aching bones?
Henceforward do your messages yourself.

65 JULIET   Here's such a coil! Come, what says Romeo?

NURSE   Have you got leave to go to shrift today?

JULIET   I have.

NURSE   Then hie you hence to Friar Lawrence' cell,
There stays a husband to make you a wife.
70   Now comes the wanton blood up in your cheeks,
They'll be in scarlet straight at any news.
Hie you to church, I must another way,
To fetch a ladder, by the which your love
Must climb a bird's nest soon when it is dark.
75   I am the drudge, and toil in your delight;
But you shall bear the burden soon at night.
Go, I'll to dinner, hie you to the cell.

JULIET   Hie to high fortune! Honest Nurse, farewell.   [*Exeunt*

Scene 6

FRIAR LAWRENCE'*s cell: enter* FRIAR LAWRENCE *and* ROMEO

FRIAR LAWRENCE   So smile the heavens upon this holy act,
That after-hours with sorrow chide us not.

ROMEO   Amen, amen! but come what sorrow can,
It cannot countervail the exchange of joy
5   That one short minute gives me in her sight.
Do thou but close our hands with holy words,
Then love-devouring Death do what he dare,

· ·

51 Beshrew your heart curse you

61 God's lady Mary, mother of God (a mild oath)

62 Are you so hot? are you so impatient

62 Marry come up, I trow An exclamation expressing indignation or surprise.

63 poultice soothing remedy

65 coil fuss

68 hie you hence go right away

70 Now comes ... cheeks now your cheeks are beginning to blush

71 be in scarlet be even brighter red

75 toil in your delight work for your happiness

76 bear the burden take responsibility; hold Romeo's body

2 That after-hours ... not that they (the heavens) won't make us pay for it later

4 countervail outweigh

It is enough I may but call her mine.

FRIAR LAWRENCE   These violent delights have violent ends,

10   And in their triumph die like fire and powder,

Which as they kiss consume. The sweetest honey

Is loathsome in his own deliciousness,

And in the taste confounds the appetite.

Therefore love moderately, long love doth so;

15   Too swift arrives as tardy as too slow.

Enter JULIET

Here comes the lady. O, so light a foot

Will ne'er wear out the everlasting flint;

A lover may bestride the gossamers

That idles in the wanton summer air,

20   And yet not fall, so light is vanity.

JULIET   Good even to my ghostly confessor.

FRIAR LAWRENCE   Romeo shall thank thee, daughter, for us both.

ROMEO *kisses* JULIET

JULIET   As much to him, else is his thanks too much.

JULIET *returns his kiss*

ROMEO   Ah, Juliet, if the measure of thy joy

25   Be heap'd like mine, and that thy skill be more

To blazon it, then sweeten with thy breath

This neighbour air, and let rich music's tongue

Unfold the imagin'd happiness that both

Receive in either by this dear encounter.

30   JULIET   Conceit, more rich in matter than in words,

Brags of his substance, not of ornament;

They are but beggars that can count their worth,

But my true love is grown to such excess

I cannot sum up sum of half my wealth.

35   FRIAR LAWRENCE   Come, come with me, and we will make short work,

For by your leaves, you shall not stay alone

Till Holy Church incorporate two in one.   [*Exeunt*

---

10 powder gunpowder

11–12 The sweetest … deliciousness the deliciousness of the sweetest honey can become disgusting

13 confounds ruins

17 flint hard stone floor

18 bestride the gossamers float on spiderwebs

20 so light is vanity that's how insubstantial worldly pleasures are

21 ghostly confessor spiritual guide

23 As much to … much. I'll have to kiss him back, or I'll owe him for the one he gave me

26 blazon it describe it in poetic detail

27 neighbour surrounding

28–29 that both … either that we bring each other

30–31 Conceit, more rich … ornament imagination runs much deeper than words; it focuses on true wealth (in love), not on fancy language

34 I cannot … wealth I can't add up the total of even half my wealth (i.e., my love)

ACT 3 Scene 1

A public place: enter MERCUTIO *and his* PAGE,
BENVOLIO *and* MEN

BENVOLIO I pray thee, good Mercutio, let's retire:
The day is hot, the Capels are abroad,
And if we meet we shall not scape a brawl,
For now, these hot days, is the mad blood stirring.

5 MERCUTIO Thou art like one of these fellows that, when he enters
the confines of a tavern, claps me his sword upon the
table, and says 'God send me no need of thee!'; and by
the operation of the second cup draws him on the
drawer, when indeed there is no need.

10 BENVOLIO Am I like such a fellow?

MERCUTIO Come, come, thou art as hot a Jack in thy mood as any
in Italy, and as soon moved to be moody, and as soon
moody to be moved.

BENVOLIO And what to?

15 MERCUTIO Nay, and there were two such, we should have none
shortly, for one would kill the other. Thou? why, thou
wilt quarrel with a man that hath a hair more or a hair
less in his beard than thou hast; thou wilt quarrel with a
man for cracking nuts, having no other reason but
20 because thou hast hazel eyes. What eye but such an eye
would spy out such a quarrel? Thy head is as full of
quarrels as an egg is full of meat, and yet thy head hath
been beaten as addle as an egg for quarrelling. Thou
hast quarrelled with a man for coughing in the street,
25 because he hath wakened thy dog that hath lain asleep
in the sun. Didst thou not fall out with a tailor for
wearing his new doublet before Easter? with another for
tying his new shoes with old riband? and yet thou wilt
tutor me from quarrelling.

30 BENVOLIO And I were so apt to quarrel as thou art, any man should
buy the fee-simple of my life for an hour and a quarter.

MERCUTIO The fee-simple? O simple!

Enter TYBALT, PETRUCHIO, *and others*

BENVOLIO By my head, here comes the Capulets.

MERCUTIO By my heel, I care not.

---

1 retire leave

2 Capels Capulets

2 abroad outside; out and about

4 these hot … stirring in hot weather like this passions run high (the play takes place in July)

7–8 by the … cup after two drinks

8–9 draws him on the drawer pulls his sword on the barman

12 as soon moved to be moody easily pushed to anger

12–13 as soon moody to be moved likely to be angry when provoked

15 and there were two such if there were two men like you

22 meat food

23 addle rotten

27 doublet A type of tight-fitting jacket.

28 riband ribbon

30 And if

30–31 any man … quarter I wouldn't expect to survive longer than an hour and a quarter

35	TYBALT	Follow me close, for I will speak to them.
		Gentlemen, good den, a word with one of you.
	MERCUTIO	And but one word with one of us? couple it with
		something, make it a word and a blow.
	TYBALT	You shall find me apt enough to that, sir, and you will
40		give me occasion.
	MERCUTIO	Could you not take some occasion without giving?
	TYBALT	Mercutio, thou consortest with Romeo.
	MERCUTIO	Consort? what, dost thou make us minstrels? And thou
		make minstrels of us, look to hear nothing but discords.
45		Here's my fiddlestick, here's that shall make you dance.
		'Zounds, consort!
	BENVOLIO	We talk here in the public haunt of men:
		Either withdraw unto some private place,
		Or reason coldly of your grievances,
50		Or else depart; here all eyes gaze on us.
	MERCUTIO	Men's eyes were made to look, and let them gaze;
		I will not budge for no man's pleasure, I.

Enter ROMEO

	TYBALT	Well, peace be with you, sir, here comes my man.
	MERCUTIO	But I'll be hang'd, sir, if he wear your livery.
55		Marry, go before to field, he'll be your follower;
		Your worship in that sense may call him man.
	TYBALT	Romeo, the love I bear thee can afford
		No better term than this: thou art a villain.
	ROMEO	Tybalt, the reason that I have to love thee
60		Doth much excuse the appertaining rage
		To such a greeting. Villain am I none;
		Therefore farewell, I see thou knowest me not.
	TYBALT	Boy, this shall not excuse the injuries
		That thou hast done me, therefore turn and draw.
65	ROMEO	I do protest I never injuried thee,
		But love thee better than thou canst devise,
		Till thou shalt know the reason of my love;
		And so, good Capulet, which name I tender
		As dearly as mine own, be satisfied.
70	MERCUTIO	O calm, dishonourable, vile submission!
		'Alla stoccata' carries it away. [*Draws*]
		Tybalt, you rat-catcher, will you walk?

37 And but only

42 consortest associate

43 Consort? a musical group

43 minstrels travelling musicians (who had little social status in Elizabethan society)

45 fiddlestick bow (Mercutio is referring to his sword)

46 'Zounds by God's wounds

49 reason coldly of your grievances work out your grievances calmly

53 my man the man I've been waiting for

54 wear your livery is your servant

55 go before to field if you lead the way to a field (for a duel)

59 the reason that I have to love thee i.e., the fact that we are now related (but Romeo can't say so)

60–61 Doth much … greeting stops me from responding to your insult with the appropriate outrage

68 tender value

71 'Alla stoccata' carries it away. Tybalt wins

72 rat-catcher A reference to Tybalt's association with cats (see note at Act 2, Scene 4, line 19).

72 will you walk will you fight

	TYBALT	What wouldst thou have with me?
	MERCUTIO	Good King of Cats, nothing but one of your nine lives
75		that I mean to make bold withal, and as you shall use
		me hereafter, dry-beat the rest of the eight. Will you
		pluck your sword out of his pilcher by the ears? Make
		haste, lest mine be about your ears ere it be out.
	TYBALT	I am for you. [*Drawing*]
80	ROMEO	Gentle Mercutio, put thy rapier up.
	MERCUTIO	Come, sir, your 'passado'.

They fight

	ROMEO	Draw, Benvolio, beat down their weapons.
		Gentlemen, for shame forbear this outrage!
		Tybalt, Mercutio, the prince expressly hath
85		Forbid this bandying in Verona streets.

ROMEO *steps between them*

Hold, Tybalt! Good Mercutio!

TYBALT *under* ROMEO*'s arm thrusts* MERCUTIO *in*

[*Away* TYBALT *with his followers*

	MERCUTIO	I am hurt.
		A plague a'both houses! I am sped.
		Is he gone and hath nothing?
	BENVOLIO	What, art thou hurt?
	MERCUTIO	Ay, ay, a scratch, a scratch, marry, 'tis enough.
90		Where is my page? Go, villain, fetch a surgeon.

[*Exit* PAGE

	ROMEO	Courage, man, the hurt cannot be much.
	MERCUTIO	No, 'tis not so deep as a well, nor so wide as a church-
		door, but 'tis enough, 'twill serve. Ask for me tomorrow,
		and you shall find me a grave man. I am peppered, I
95		warrant, for this world. A plague a'both your houses!
		'Zounds, a dog, a rat, a mouse, a cat, to scratch a man to
		death! a braggart, a rogue, a villain, that fights by the
		book of arithmetic. Why the dev'l came you between us!
		I was hurt under your arm.
100	ROMEO	I thought all for the best.
	MERCUTIO	Help me into some house, Benvolio,
		Or I shall faint. A plague a'both your houses!

. . . .

75 that I … withal that I will do whatever I want with (cats were said to have nine lives)

75–76 use me treat me

76 dry-beat pummel; hit without drawing blood

77 pilcher sheath

77 by the ears against its will

78 about your ears hitting you

83 forebear this outrage stop this stupidity

86 s.d. thrusts Mercutio in stabs Mercutio

87 I am sped. I'm dispatched

88 hath nothing with no injuries

90 villain fellow (not an insult in this context)

93 'twill serve it'll do; it's enough

94 a grave man a serious fellow; a dead man

94–95 I am peppered … world. I guess I'm ruined for this world

97–98 that fights … arithmetic who fights without passion

They have made worms' meat of me. I have it,
And soundly too. Your houses!   [*Exit with* BENVOLIO

105 ROMEO   This gentleman, the prince's near ally,
My very friend, hath got his mortal hurt
In my behalf; my reputation stain'd
With Tybalt's slander—Tybalt, that an hour
Hath been my cousin. O sweet Juliet,
110   Thy beauty hath made me effeminate,
And in my temper soften'd valour's steel!

Enter BENVOLIO

BENVOLIO O Romeo, Romeo, brave Mercutio is dead.
That gallant spirit hath aspir'd the clouds,
Which too untimely here did scorn the earth.

115 ROMEO   This day's black fate on moe days doth depend,
This but begins the woe others must end.

Enter TYBALT

BENVOLIO Here comes the furious Tybalt back again.

ROMEO   Again, in triumph, and Mercutio slain?
Away to heaven, respective lenity,
120   And fire-ey'd fury be my conduct now!
Now, Tybalt, take the 'villain' back again
That late thou gavest me, for Mercutio's soul
Is but a little way above our heads,
Staying for thine to keep him company:
125   Either thou or I, or both, must go with him.

TYBALT   Thou wretched boy, that didst consort him here,
Shalt with him hence.

ROMEO   This shall determine that.

They fight; TYBALT *falls*

BENVOLIO Romeo, away, be gone!
The citizens are up, and Tybalt slain.
130   Stand not amaz'd, the prince will doom thee death
If thou art taken. Hence be gone, away!

ROMEO   O, I am fortune's fool.

BENVOLIO   Why dost thou stay?   [*Exit* ROMEO

Enter CITIZENS *and* OFFICERS *of the Watch*

103–104 I have it, and soundly too. I've had it, that's for sure

105 near ally close relative

106–107 hath got … behalf has been mortally wounded on my account

111 And in … steel and made me soft

113 aspir'd ascended to

114 Which too … earth who left this earth too soon

115 This day's … depend the outcome of these events will depend on what happens in days to come (moe: more)

119 Away to … lenity forget about being considerate and lenient (toward Tybalt)

121 take the 'villain' back again Romeo is referring to the insult Tybalt threw at him at line 58.

126 consort spend time with

129 up awake; angry

130 Stand not amaz'd don't stand there looking stunned

OFFICER   Which way ran he that kill'd Mercutio?
           Tybalt, that murderer, which way ran he?

135 BENVOLIO There lies that Tybalt.

OFFICER   Up, sir, go with me;
           I charge thee in the prince's name obey.

Enter PRINCE, *old* MONTAGUE, CAPULET, *their* WIVES, *and all*

PRINCE   Where are the vile beginners of this fray?

BENVOLIO   O noble prince, I can discover all
           The unlucky manage of this fatal brawl;
140   There lies the man, slain by young Romeo,
           That slew thy kinsman, brave Mercutio.

LADY CAPULET   Tybalt, my cousin! O my brother's child!
           O Prince! O husband! O, the blood is spill'd
           Of my dear kinsman. Prince, as thou art true,
145   For blood of ours, shed blood of Montague.
           O cousin, cousin!

PRINCE   Benvolio, who began this bloody fray?

BENVOLIO   Tybalt, here slain, whom Romeo's hand did slay.
           Romeo, that spoke him fair, bid him bethink
150   How nice the quarrel was, and urg'd withal
           Your high displeasure; all this, uttered
           With gentle breath, calm look, knees humbly bow'd,
           Could not take truce with the unruly spleen
           Of Tybalt deaf to peace, but that he tilts
155   With piercing steel at bold Mercutio's breast,
           Who, all as hot, turns deadly point to point,
           And with a martial scorn, with one hand beats
           Cold death aside, and with the other sends
           It back to Tybalt, whose dexterity
160   Retorts it. Romeo he cries aloud,
           'Hold, friends! friends, part!' and swifter than his tongue,
           His agile arm beats down their fatal points,
           And 'twixt them rushes; underneath whose arm
           An envious thrust from Tybalt hit the life
165   Of stout Mercutio, and then Tybalt fled;
           But by and by comes back to Romeo,
           Who had but newly entertain'd revenge,
           And to't they go like lightning, for, ere I
           Could draw to part them, was stout Tybalt slain;
170   And as he fell, did Romeo turn and fly.

- -

137 fray fight

138 discover explain

139 manage course

149 spoke him fair was polite to him

149 bethink consider

150 nice trivial; unimportant

150 urg'd withal also pointed out

153 Could not take truce couldn't pacify

153 unruly spleen unregulated temper

154 but that just the opposite

156 all as hot just as angry

157 martial warlike

157–158 with one … aside with one hand defends himself again Tybalt's blows

160 Retorts it sends it back

163 'twixt between

164 envious malicious

165 stout brave

167 entertain'd considered

This is the truth, or let Benvolio die.

LADY CAPULET He is a kinsman to the Montague,
Affection makes him false, he speaks not true:
Some twenty of them fought in this black strife,
175   And all those twenty could but kill one life.
I beg for justice, which thou, Prince, must give:
Romeo slew Tybalt, Romeo must not live.

PRINCE Romeo slew him, he slew Mercutio;
Who now the price of his dear blood doth owe?

180 MONTAGUE Not Romeo, Prince, he was Mercutio's friend;
His fault concludes but what the law should end,
The life of Tybalt.

PRINCE   And for that offence
Immediately we do exile him hence.
I have an interest in your hearts' proceeding:
185   My blood for your rude brawls doth lie a-bleeding;
But I'll amerce you with so strong a fine
That you shall all repent the loss of mine.
I will be deaf to pleading and excuses,
Nor tears nor prayers shall purchase out abuses:
190   Therefore use none. Let Romeo hence in haste,
Else, when he is found, that hour is his last.
Bear hence this body, and attend our will:
Mercy but murders, pardoning those that kill.   [Exeunt

Scene 2

CAPULET's *house: enter* JULIET *alone*

JULIET   Gallop apace, you fiery-footed steeds,
Towards Phoebus' lodging; such a waggoner
As Phaëton would whip you to the west,
And bring in cloudy night immediately.
5   Spread thy close curtain, love-performing Night,
That runaways' eyes may wink, and Romeo
Leap to these arms, untalk'd of and unseen:
Lovers can see to do their amorous rites
By their own beauties, or if love be blind,
10   It best agrees with night. Come, civil Night,
Thou sober-suited matron all in black,
And learn me how to lose a winning match,
Play'd for a pair of stainless maidenhoods.

....

181 His fault ... end he only killed someone who should have been sentenced to death anyway

184 in your hearts' proceeding in the results of your emotional outbursts

185 My blood i.e., Mercutio

186 amerce punish

189 purchase out make amends for

193 Mercy but ... kill pardoning murderers will only encourage more murders

1 apace swiftly

1 fiery-footed steeds A reference to the horses drawing the chariot of the sun god, Phoebus Apollo.

2 Phoebus' lodging the west (where the sun sets)

3 Phaëton The son of Phoebus. He stole his father's chariot and tried to ride it across the sky.

5 close curtain A curtain around a bed.

5 love-performing Night night, the time when acts of love are performed

6 wink close; pretend not to see

12 learn me ... match teach me how to lose my virginity, while gaining a husband

Hood my unmann'd blood, bating in my cheeks,

15 With thy black mantle, till strange love grow bold,

Think true love acted simple modesty.

Come, Night, come, Romeo, come, thou day in night,

For thou wilt lie upon the wings of night,

Whiter than new snow upon a raven's back.

20 Come, gentle Night, come, loving, black-brow'd Night,

Give me my Romeo, and when I shall die,

Take him and cut him out in little stars,

And he will make the face of heaven so fine

That all the world will be in love with night,

25 And pay no worship to the garish sun.

O, I have bought the mansion of a love,

But not possess'd it, and though I am sold,

Not yet enjoy'd. So tedious is this day

As is the night before some festival

30 To an impatient child that hath new robes

And may not wear them. O, here comes my Nurse,

Enter NURSE, *with the ladder of cords in her lap*

And she brings news, and every tongue that speaks

But Romeo's name speaks heavenly eloquence.

Now, Nurse, what news? What hast thou there? the cords

35 That Romeo bid thee fetch?

NURSE   Ay, ay, the cords.

Throws them down

JULIET   Ay me, what news? Why dost thou wring thy hands?

NURSE   Ah weraday, he's dead, he's dead, he's dead!

We are undone, lady, we are undone.

Alack the day, he's gone, he's kill'd, he's dead!

40 JULIET   Can heaven be so envious?

NURSE   Romeo can,

Though heaven cannot. O Romeo, Romeo!

Who ever would have thought it? Romeo!

JULIET   What devil are thou that dost torment me thus?

This torture should be roar'd in dismal hell.

45 Hath Romeo slain himself? Say thou but 'ay',

And that bare vowel 'I' shall poison more

Than the death-darting eye of cockatrice.

I am not I, if there be such an 'ay',

14–15 Hood my ... mantle cover my blushing cheeks with your darkness

15 strange shy

16 Think true ... modesty and believe that sex between true lovers is pure and good

27–28 though I ... enjoy'd though I belong to someone else now (i.e., Romeo), he has not taken possession yet

31 s.d. cords The rope ladder, which Romeo requested in Act 2, Scene 4, line 172.

37 weraday alas

38 undone destroyed

40 envious malicious

45–47 Say thou ... cockatrice. Juliet puns on "ay" (yes), "I," and "eye." A cockatrice was a mythological creature, half serpent, half rooster, whose look could kill.

	Or those eyes shut, that makes thee answer 'ay'.
50	If he be slain, say 'ay', or if not, 'no':
	Brief sounds determine my weal or woe.
NURSE	I saw the wound, I saw it with mine eyes
	(God save the mark!), here on his manly breast:
	A piteous corse, a bloody piteous corse,
55	Pale, pale as ashes, all bedaub'd in blood,
	All in gore blood; I sounded at the sight.
JULIET	O break, my heart, poor bankrout, break at once!
	To prison, eyes, ne'er look on liberty!
	Vile earth, to earth resign, end motion here,
60	And thou and Romeo press one heavy bier!
NURSE	O Tybalt, Tybalt, the best friend I had!
	O courteous Tybalt, honest gentleman,
	That ever I should live to see thee dead!
JULIET	What storm is this that blows so contrary?
65	Is Romeo slaughter'd? and is Tybalt dead?
	My dearest cousin, and my dearer lord?
	Then, dreadful trumpet, sound the general doom,
	For who is living, if those two are gone?
NURSE	Tybalt is gone and Romeo banished,
70	Romeo that kill'd him, he is banished.
JULIET	O God, did Romeo's hand shed Tybalt's blood?
NURSE	It did, it did, alas the day, it did!
JULIET	O serpent heart, hid with a flow'ring face!
	Did ever dragon keep so fair a cave?
75	Beautiful tyrant, fiend angelical!
	Dove-feather'd raven, wolvish-ravening lamb!
	Despised substance of divinest show!
	Just opposite to what thou justly seem'st,
	A damned saint, an honourable villain!
80	O nature, what hadst thou to do in hell
	When thou didst bower the spirit of a fiend
	In mortal paradise of such sweet flesh?
	Was ever book containing such vile matter
	So fairly bound? O that deceit should dwell
85	In such a gorgeous palace!
NURSE	There's no trust,
	No faith, no honesty in men, all perjur'd,
	All forsworn, all naught, all dissemblers.

---

51 weal well-being

54 corse corpse

55 bedaub'd spattered

56 sounded fainted

57 bankrout bankrupt

59 Vile earth, to earth resign my earthly body, surrender yourself to the ground

60 press one heavy bier lie in the same grave

67 dreadful trumpet The last trumpet, which according to the Christian Bible will sound on the Day of Judgement.

76 wolvish-ravening lamb lamb that attacks like a wolf

77 Despised substance ... show! despised being that appears so divine

81–82 bower the ... flesh hide a devil in such a sweet body

86 perjur'd oath-breakers

87 forsworn untrue to their vows

87 naught wicked

Ah, where's my man? Give me some aqua-vitae;
These griefs, these woes, these sorrows make me old.

90   Shame come to Romeo!

JULIET   Blister'd be thy tongue
For such a wish! he was not born to shame:
Upon his brow shame is asham'd to sit;
For 'tis a throne where honour may be crown'd
Sole monarch of the universal earth.

95   O what a beast was I to chide at him!

NURSE   Will you speak well of him that kill'd your cousin?

JULIET   Shall I speak ill of him that is my husband?
Ah, poor my lord, what tongue shall smooth thy name,
When I, thy three-hours wife, have mangl'd it?

100   But wherefore, villain, didst thou kill my cousin?
That villain cousin would have kill'd my husband.
Back, foolish tears, back to your native spring,
Your tributary drops belong to woe,
Which you mistaking offer up to joy.

105   My husband lives that Tybalt would have slain,
And Tybalt's dead that would have slain my husband:
All this is comfort, wherefore weep I then?
Some word there was, worser than Tybalt's death,
That murder'd me; I would forget it fain,

110   But O, it presses to my memory,
Like damned guilty deeds to sinners' minds:
'Tybalt is dead, and Romeo banished.'
That 'banished', that one word 'banished',
Hath slain ten thousand Tybalts. Tybalt's death

115   Was woe enough if it had ended there;
Or if sour woe delights in fellowship,
And needly will be rank'd with other griefs,
Why follow'd not, when she said 'Tybalt's dead',
'Thy father' or 'thy mother', nay, or both,

120   Which modern lamentation might have mov'd?
But with a rear-ward following Tybalt's death,
'Romeo is banished': to speak that word,
Is father, mother, Tybalt, Romeo, Juliet,
All slain, all dead. 'Romeo is banished!'

125   There is no end, no limit, measure, bound,
In that word's death, no words can that woe sound.
Where is my father and my mother, Nurse?

. . . .

88 aqua-vitae brandy

95 chide at scold

103 tributary drops tears of tribute

104 Which you ... joy which you are mistakenly offering at a time of joy (because Romeo is alive)

105 would have slain tried to kill

109 fain gladly

117 needly will ... griefs must be followed by other tragedies (i.e., if sorrows must come in groups)

120 Which modern ... mov'd which would have called for ordinary grieving

121 rear-ward a second assault, taking me unawares

126 In that word's death in the destruction that word brings

	NURSE	Weeping and wailing over Tybalt's corse.
		Will you go to them? I will bring you thither.
130	JULIET	Wash they his wounds with tears? mine shall be spent,
		When theirs are dry, for Romeo's banishment.
		Take up those cords. Poor ropes, you are beguil'd,
		Both you and I, for Romeo is exil'd.
		He made you for a highway to my bed,
135		But I, a maid, die maiden-widowed.
		Come, cords, come, Nurse, I'll to my wedding bed,
		And death, not Romeo, take my maidenhead!
	NURSE	Hie to your chamber. I'll find Romeo
		To comfort you, I wot well where he is.
140		Hark ye, your Romeo will be here at night.
		I'll to him, he is hid at Lawrence' cell.
	JULIET	O find him! Give this ring to my true knight,
		And bid him come to take his last farewell.

[*Exeunt*

Scene 3

FRIAR LAWRENCE'*s cell: enter* FRIAR LAWRENCE

	FRIAR LAWRENCE	Romeo, come forth, come forth, thou fearful man:
		Affliction is enamour'd of thy parts,
		And thou art wedded to calamity.

Enter ROMEO

	ROMEO	Father, what news? What is the prince's doom?
5		What sorrow craves acquaintance at my hand,
		That I yet know not?
	FRIAR LAWRENCE	Too familiar
		Is my dear son with such sour company!
		I bring thee tidings of the prince's doom.
	ROMEO	What less than doomsday is the prince's doom?
10	FRIAR LAWRENCE	A gentler judgement vanish'd from his lips:
		Not body's death, but body's banishment.
	ROMEO	Ha, banishment? be merciful, say 'death':
		For exile hath more terror in his look,
		Much more than death. Do not say 'banishment'!
15	FRIAR LAWRENCE	Here from Verona art thou banished.
		Be patient, for the world is broad and wide.
	ROMEO	There is no world without Verona walls,

---

132 beguil'd tricked
135 I, a maid, die maiden-widowed
I will die both a virgin and a widow
137 maidenhead virginity

139 wot know
1 fearful frightened; scared
2 Affliction is ... parts distress is in love with your whole being

4 doom judgment
8 tidings news
10 vanish'd from flew from

13 exile hath more terror in his look
exile looks scarier to me (than death)
17 without beyond

But purgatory, torture, hell itself:

Hence 'banished' is banish'd from the world,

20   And world's exile is death; then 'banished'

Is death misterm'd. Calling death 'banished',

Thou cut'st my head off with a golden axe,

And smilest upon the stroke that murders me.

FRIAR LAWRENCE O deadly sin! O rude unthankfulness!

25   Thy fault our law calls death, but the kind prince,

Taking thy part, hath rush'd aside the law,

And turn'd that black word 'death' to 'banishment'.

This is dear mercy, and thou seest it not.

ROMEO   'Tis torture, and not mercy. Heaven is here

30   Where Juliet lives, and every cat and dog

And little mouse, every unworthy thing,

Live here in heaven, and may look on her,

But Romeo may not. More validity,

More honourable state, more courtship lives

35   In carrion flies than Romeo; they may seize

On the white wonder of dear Juliet's hand,

And steal immortal blessing from her lips,

Who even in pure and vestal modesty

Still blush, as thinking their own kisses sin;

40   But Romeo may not, he is banished.

Flies may do this, but I from this must fly;

They are free men, but I am banished:

And sayest thou yet that exile is not death?

Hadst thou no poison mix'd, no sharp-ground knife,

45   No sudden mean of death, though ne'er so mean,

But 'banished' to kill me? 'Banished'?

O Friar, the damned use that word in hell;

Howling attends it. How hast thou the heart,

Being a divine, a ghostly confessor,

50   A sin-absolver, and my friend profess'd,

To mangle me with that word 'banished'?

FRIAR LAWRENCE Thou fond mad man, hear me a little speak.

ROMEO   O thou wilt speak again of banishment.

FRIAR LAWRENCE I'll give thee armour to keep off that word:

55   Adversity's sweet milk, philosophy,

To comfort thee though thou art banished.

ROMEO   Yet 'banished'? Hang up philosophy!

---

18 purgatory In Catholic theology, the place where souls suffered for their earthly sins to earn a place in heaven.

21 death misterm'd just another name for death

22 Thou cut'st ... axe i.e., banishment may look like a better fate, but they both mean death to me

25 Thy fault our law calls death the sentence for your crime is normally death

26 rush'd aside brushed aside

34 courtship courtly behaviour

35 carrion flies flies that eat corpses

38 vestal virginal

39 Still blush ... sin are forever blushing, because they (her lips) touch each other (i.e., kiss)

44–46 Hadst thou ... me? couldn't you have used poison, or a sharp knife, or some other quick way to kill me, no matter how unworthy, rather than the word "banished"

49 divine priest

52 fond silly

55 Adversity's sweet milk comfort in times of trouble

57 Yet 'banished'? are you still using that word, "banished"

57 Hang up give up

Unless philosophy can make a Juliet,
Displant a town, reverse a prince's doom,
60   It helps not, it prevails not; talk no more.

FRIAR LAWRENCE   O then I see that mad men have no ears.

ROMEO   How should they when that wise men have no eyes?

FRIAR LAWRENCE   Let me dispute with thee of thy estate.

ROMEO   Thou canst not speak of that thou dost not feel.
65   Wert thou as young as I, Juliet thy love,
An hour but married, Tybalt murdered,
Doting like me, and like me banished,
Then mightst thou speak, then mightst thou tear thy hair,
And fall upon the ground as I do now,
70   Taking the measure of an unmade grave.

Enter NURSE *within and knock*

FRIAR LAWRENCE   Arise, one knocks. Good Romeo, hide thyself.

ROMEO   Not I, unless the breath of heart-sick groans
Mist-like infold me from the search of eyes.

Knock

FRIAR LAWRENCE   Hark how they knock!—Who's there?—Romeo, arise,
75   Thou wilt be taken.—Stay a while!—Stand up;

Loud knock

Run to my study.—By and by!—God's will,
What simpleness is this?—I come, I come!

Knock

Who knocks so hard? whence come you? what's your will?

NURSE   [*Within*] Let me come in, and you shall know my errand:
80   I come from Lady Juliet.

FRIAR LAWRENCE   Welcome then.

Unlocks the door

Enter NURSE

NURSE   O holy Friar, O tell me, holy Friar,
Where's my lady's lord? where's Romeo?

FRIAR LAWRENCE   There on the ground, with his own tears made drunk.

NURSE   O he is even in my mistress' case,
85   Just in her case. O woeful sympathy!

---

59 Displant move

60 it prevails not it's useless

61 have no ears are unwilling to listen to good advice

62 have no eyes can't see the real situation in front of them

63 Let me … estate. let's discuss your situation rationally

67 Doting madly in love

70 Taking the … grave getting ready to die

73 infold me hide me

75 taken arrested

77 simpleness foolishness

84 he is even in my mistress' case he's in the same state as my mistress

Piteous predicament! even so lies she,
Blubb'ring and weeping, weeping and blubb'ring.
Stand up, stand up, stand, and you be a man;
For Juliet's sake, for her sake, rise and stand;
90 Why should you fall into so deep an O?

ROMEO Nurse!

He rises

NURSE Ah, sir, ah, sir, death's the end of all.

ROMEO Spakest thou of Juliet? how is it with her?
Doth not she think me an old murderer,
95 Now I have stain'd the childhood of our joy
With blood remov'd but little from her own?
Where is she? and how doth she? and what says
My conceal'd lady to our cancell'd love?

NURSE O she says nothing, sir, but weeps and weeps,
100 And now falls on her bed, and then starts up,
And Tybalt calls, and then on Romeo cries,
And then down falls again.

ROMEO   As if that name,
Shot from the deadly level of a gun,
Did murder her, as that name's cursed hand
105 Murder'd her kinsman. O tell me, Friar, tell me,
In what vile part of this anatomy
Doth my name lodge? Tell me, that I may sack
The hateful mansion.

He offers to stab himself, and NURSE *snatches the dagger away*

FRIAR LAWRENCE   Hold thy desperate hand!
Art thou a man? thy form cries out thou art;
110 Thy tears are womanish, thy wild acts denote
The unreasonable fury of a beast.
Unseemly woman in a seeming man,
And ill-beseeming beast in seeming both,
Thou hast amaz'd me. By my holy order,
115 I thought thy disposition better temper'd.
Hast thou slain Tybalt? wilt thou slay thyself,
And slay thy lady that in thy life lives,
By doing damned hate upon thyself?
Why rail'st thou on thy birth? the heaven and earth?

90 **so deep an O** so much wailing
93 **how is it with her** how is she
96 **blood remov'd … own** a close relative of hers
98 **conceal'd lady** secret wife
107–108 **that I … mansion** so that I can attack the horrible place (where my name lives)
112 **Unseemly** improper
113 **ill-beseeming beast … both** i.e., by acting like a woman while looking like a man, you become a monstrous beast
117 **that in thy life lives** who lives for you
118 **doing damned hate upon thyself** doing harm to yourself
119 **rail'st** rage; rant

120   Since birth, and heaven, and earth, all three do meet
      In thee at once, which thou at once wouldst lose.
      Fie, fie, thou sham'st thy shape, thy love, thy wit,
      Which like a usurer abound'st in all,
      And usest none in that true use indeed
125   Which should bedeck thy shape, thy love, thy wit:
      Thy noble shape is but a form of wax,
      Digressing from the valour of a man;
      Thy dear love sworn but hollow perjury,
      Killing that love which thou hast vow'd to cherish;
130   Thy wit, that ornament to shape and love,
      Misshapen in the conduct of them both,
      Like powder in a skilless soldier's flask,
      Is set afire by thine own ignorance,
      And thou dismember'd with thine own defence.
135   What, rouse thee, man! thy Juliet is alive,
      For whose dear sake thou wast but lately dead:
      There art thou happy. Tybalt would kill thee,
      But thou slewest Tybalt: there art thou happy.
      The law that threaten'd death becomes thy friend,
140   And turns it to exile: there art thou happy.
      A pack of blessings light upon thy back,
      Happiness courts thee in her best array,
      But like a mishaved and sullen wench,
      Thou pouts upon thy fortune and thy love:
145   Take heed, take heed, for such die miserable.
      Go get thee to thy love as was decreed,
      Ascend her chamber, hence and comfort her;
      But look thou stay not till the Watch be set,
      For then thou canst not pass to Mantua,
150   Where thou shalt live till we can find a time
      To blaze your marriage, reconcile your friends,
      Beg pardon of the prince, and call thee back
      With twenty hundred thousand times more joy
      Than thou went'st forth in lamentation.
155   Go before, Nurse, commend me to thy lady,
      And bid her hasten all the house to bed,
      Which heavy sorrow makes them apt unto.
      Romeo is coming.

NURSE   O Lord, I could have stay'd here all the night
160   To hear good counsel. O, what learning is!

··

120–121 birth, and … once these three things make you who you are: your birth (i.e., your social background), your soul, and your body

123 like a usurer like a money lender (who has lots of money, but uses it in an immoral way)

126 Thy noble … wax you look like a noble man, but you're a fake (like a waxwork figure)

127 Digressing from … man without true manly courage

128 hollow perjury empty promises

131 Misshapen in … both misguided in how they guide your actions

132 powder gunpowder

132 flask container

136 For whose … dead for whose sake you just tried to kill yourself

137 happy lucky

142 array fine clothing

143 mishaved misbehaved

148 till the Watch be set till the night guard is on duty

151 blaze proclaim

157 apt unto ready to agree to

My lord, I'll tell my lady you will come.

ROMEO   Do so, and bid my sweet prepare to chide.

NURSE offers to go in, and turns again

NURSE   Here, sir, a ring she bid me give you, sir.

Hie you, make haste, for it grows very late.

165 ROMEO   How well my comfort is revived by this.   *[Exit NURSE*

FRIAR LAWRENCE   Go hence, good night, and here stands all your state:

Either be gone before the Watch be set,

Or by the break of day disguis'd from hence.

Sojourn in Mantua; I'll find out your man,

170   And he shall signify from time to time

Every good hap to you that chances here.

Give me thy hand, 'tis late. Farewell, good night.

ROMEO   But that a joy past joy calls out on me,

It were a grief, so brief to part with thee:

175   Farewell.   *[Exeunt*

Scene 4

*Monday late evening: CAPULET's house. Enter old
CAPULET, his WIFE, and PARIS*

CAPULET   Things have fall'n out, sir, so unluckily

That we have had no time to move our daughter.

Look you, she lov'd her kinsman Tybalt dearly,

And so did I. Well, we were born to die.

5   'Tis very late, she'll not come down tonight.

I promise you, but for your company,

I would have been abed an hour ago.

PARIS   These times of woe afford no times to woo.

Madam, good night, commend me to your daughter.

10 LADY CAPULET   I will, and know her mind early tomorrow;

Tonight she's mew'd up to her heaviness.

PARIS offers to go in, and CAPULET calls him again

CAPULET   Sir Paris, I will make a desperate tender

Of my child's love: I think she will be rul'd

In all respects by me; nay more, I doubt it not.

15   Wife, go you to her ere you go to bed,

Acquaint her here of my son Paris' love,

---

162 chide scold me

166 here stands all your state your life depends on this

169 find out your man contact your servant

170 signify report

171 Every good hap every good bit of news

173 But that except for the fact that

174 It were … thee it would be a pity to be so curt in saying goodbye to you

2 move persuade

11 mew'd up to her heaviness imprisoned by sorrow

12 desperate tender bold proposal

16 my son my son-in-law

And bid her—mark you me?—on Wednesday next—
But soft, what day is this?

PARIS   Monday my lord.

CAPULET   Monday, ha, ha! Well, Wednesday is too soon,
20   A'Thursday let it be—a'Thursday, tell her,
            She shall be married to this noble earl.
            Will you be ready? do you like this haste?
            Well, keep no great ado—a friend or two,
            For hark you, Tybalt being slain so late,
25   It may be thought we held him carelessly,
            Being our kinsman, if we revel much:
            Therefore we'll have some half a dozen friends,
            And there an end. But what say you to Thursday?

PARIS   My lord, I would that Thursday were tomorrow.

30 CAPULET Well, get you gone, a'Thursday be it then.—
            Go you to Juliet ere you go to bed,
            Prepare her, wife, against this wedding day.
            Farewell, my lord. Light to my chamber, ho!
            Afore me, it is so very late that we
35   May call it early by and by. Good night.   [Exeunt

Scene 5

Very early Tuesday morning: JULIET's *bedroom. Enter*
ROMEO *and* JULIET *aloft as at the window*

JULIET   Wilt thou be gone? It is not yet near day:
            It was the nightingale, and not the lark,
            That pierc'd the fearful hollow of thine ear;
            Nightly she sings on yond pomegranate tree.
5   Believe me, love, it was the nightingale.

ROMEO   It was the lark, the herald of the morn,
            No nightingale. Look, love, what envious streaks
            Do lace the severing clouds in yonder east:
            Night's candles are burnt out, and jocund day
10   Stands tiptoe on the misty mountain tops.
            I must be gone and live, or stay and die.

JULIET   Yond light is not daylight, I know it, I:
            It is some meteor that the sun exhal'd
            To be to thee this night a torch-bearer,
15   And light thee on thy way to Mantua.

---

17 mark you me are you listening

23 keep no great ado don't make it a big event

25 held him carelessly thought of him indifferently

34 Afore me I declare

2 nightingale A bird that sings at night.

2 lark A bird that begins singing in the early morning, before dawn.

8 severing breaking

9 jocund joyful

13 some meteor that the sun exhal'd Meteors were thought to be caused by earthly vapours set alight by the sun.

Therefore stay yet, thou need'st not to be gone.

ROMEO Let me be tane, let me be put to death,
I am content, so thou wilt have it so.
I'll say yon grey is not the morning's eye,
20 'Tis but the pale reflex of Cynthia's brow;
Nor that is not the lark whose notes do beat
The vaulty heaven so high above our heads.
I have more care to stay than will to go:
Come, death, and welcome! Juliet wills it so.
25 How is't, my soul? Let's talk, it is not day.

JULIET It is, it is, hie hence, be gone, away!
It is the lark that sings so out of tune,
Straining harsh discords and unpleasing sharps.
Some say the lark makes sweet division:
30 This doth not so, for she divideth us.
Some say the lark and loathed toad chang'd eyes;
O now I would they had chang'd voices too,
Since arm from arm that voice doth us affray,
Hunting thee hence with hunt's-up to the day.
35 O now be gone, more light and light it grows.

ROMEO More light and light, more dark and dark our woes!

Enter NURSE *hastily*

NURSE Madam!

JULIET Nurse?

NURSE Your lady mother is coming to your chamber.
40 The day is broke, be wary, look about.   [*Exit*

JULIET Then, window, let day in, and let life out.

ROMEO Farewell, farewell! one kiss, and I'll descend.

He goeth down

JULIET Art thou gone so, love, lord, ay husband, friend?
I must hear from thee every day in the hour,
45 For in a minute there are many days.
O, by this count I shall be much in years
Ere I again behold my Romeo!

ROMEO [*From below*] Farewell!
I will omit no opportunity
50 That may convey my greetings, love, to thee.

JULIET O think'st thou we shall ever meet again?

....

17 tane taken

20 pale reflex of Cynthia's brow
reflection of the moon

23 care desire

29 sweet division beautiful music
(with a pun on "divideth" in line 30)

31 Some say ... eyes A reference to
a popular belief.

33 arm from ... affray the voice (of
the lark) scares us from each other's
arms

34 Hunting thee ... day forcing you
to flee as if the daylight were hunting
you

46 much in years much older; aged

	ROMEO	I doubt it not, and all these woes shall serve
		For sweet discourses in our times to come.
	JULIET	O God, I have an ill-divining soul!
55		Methinks I see thee now, thou art so low,
		As one dead in the bottom of a tomb.
		Either my eyesight fails, or thou look'st pale.
	ROMEO	And trust me, love, in my eye so do you:
		Dry sorrow drinks our blood. Adieu, adieu! [*Exit*
60	JULIET	O Fortune, Fortune, all men call thee fickle;
		If thou art fickle, what dost thou with him
		That is renown'd for faith? Be fickle, Fortune:
		For then I hope thou wilt not keep him long,
		But send him back.

Enter mother, LADY CAPULET, below

	LADY CAPULET	Ho, daughter, are you up?
65	JULIET	Who is't that calls? It is my lady mother.
		Is she not down so late, or up so early?
		What unaccustom'd cause procures her hither?

She goeth down from the window and enters below

	LADY CAPULET	Why how now, Juliet?
	JULIET	Madam, I am not well.
	LADY CAPULET	Evermore weeping for your cousin's death?
70		What, wilt thou wash him from his grave with tears?
		And if thou couldst, thou couldst not make him live;
		Therefore have done. Some grief shows much of love,
		But much of grief shows still some want of wit.
	JULIET	Yet let me weep for such a feeling loss.
75	LADY CAPULET	So shall you feel the loss, but not the friend
		Which you weep for.
	JULIET	Feeling so the loss,
		I cannot choose but ever weep the friend.
	LADY CAPULET	Well, girl, thou weep'st not so much for his death
		As that the villain lives which slaughter'd him.
80	JULIET	What villain, madam?
	LADY CAPULET	That same villain Romeo.
	JULIET	[*Aside*] Villain and he be many miles asunder.—
		God pardon him, I do with all my heart:
		And yet no man like he doth grieve my heart.

. . . .

59 Dry sorrow drinks our blood. Elizabethans believed sadness made people lose blood (a drop per sigh) and therefore look pale.

60 fickle changeable; capricious

61 what dost thou with what do you have to do with

66 Is she not down so late is she staying up so late

67 procures her hither brings her here

68 how now what's wrong

72 have done give it up

73 much of … wit grieving too much makes you look foolish

74 feeling heartfelt

75 So shall … friend you're grieving for its own sake, not for Tybalt's

76–77 Feeling so … friend. Juliet is secretly thinking of Romeo, not Tybalt.

81 Villain and … asunder. he's far from being a villain

83 no man … heart no man causes me as much grief as he; someone like him could never cause me grief

LADY CAPULET   That is because the traitor murderer lives.

85 JULIET   Ay, madam, from the reach of these my hands.
            Would none but I might venge my cousin's death!

LADY CAPULET   We will have vengeance for it, fear thou not:
            Then weep no more. I'll send to one in Mantua,
            Where that same banish'd runagate doth live,
90   Shall give him such an unaccustom'd dram
            That he shall soon keep Tybalt company;
            And then I hope thou wilt be satisfied.

JULIET   Indeed I never shall be satisfied
            With Romeo, till I behold him—dead—
95   Is my poor heart, so for a kinsman vex'd.
            Madam, if you could find out but a man
            To bear a poison, I would temper it,
            That Romeo should upon receipt thereof
            Soon sleep in quiet. O how my heart abhors
100   To hear him nam'd and cannot come to him,
            To wreak the love I bore my cousin
            Upon his body that hath slaughter'd him!

LADY CAPULET   Find thou the means, and I'll find such a man.
            But now I'll tell thee joyful tidings, girl.

105 JULIET   And joy comes well in such a needy time.
            What are they, beseech your ladyship?

LADY CAPULET   Well, well, thou hast a careful father, child,
            One who, to put thee from thy heaviness,
            Hath sorted out a sudden day of joy,
110   That thou expects not, nor I look'd not for.

JULIET   Madam, in happy time, what day is that?

LADY CAPULET   Marry, my child, early next Thursday morn,
            The gallant, young, and noble gentleman,
            The County Paris, at Saint Peter's Church,
115   Shall happily make thee there a joyful bride.

JULIET   Now by Saint Peter's Church and Peter too,
            He shall not make me there a joyful bride.
            I wonder at this haste, that I must wed
            Ere he that should be husband comes to woo.
120   I pray you tell my lord and father, madam,
            I will not marry yet, and when I do, I swear
            It shall be Romeo, whom you know I hate,
            Rather than Paris. These are news indeed!

· ·

86 Would I wish

89 runagate vagabond

90 dram drink (poison)

95 vex'd upset

96 find out but a man just find someone

97 temper it mix it; dilute it

101 wreak avenge; unleash

107 careful thoughtful; caring

108 heaviness sadness

109 sorted out a sudden arranged an unexpected

119 should be wants to be

LADY CAPULET   Here comes your father, tell him so yourself;
125   And see how he will take it at your hands.

Enter CAPULET *and* NURSE

CAPULET   When the sun sets, the earth doth drizzle dew,
                   But for the sunset of my brother's son
                   It rains downright.
                   How now, a conduit, girl? What, still in tears?
130   Evermore show'ring? In one little body
                   Thou counterfeits a bark, a sea, a wind:
                   For still thy eyes, which I may call the sea,
                   Do ebb and flow with tears; the bark thy body is,
                   Sailing in this salt flood; the winds, thy sighs,
135   Who, raging with thy tears and they with them,
                   Without a sudden calm, will overset
                   Thy tempest-tossed body. How now, wife,
                   Have you deliver'd to her our decree?

LADY CAPULET   Ay, sir, but she will none, she gives you thanks.
140   I would the fool were married to her grave.

CAPULET   Soft, take me with you, take me with you, wife.
                   How, will she none? doth she not give us thanks?
                   Is she not proud? doth she not count her blest,
                   Unworthy as she is, that we have wrought
145   So worthy a gentleman to be her bride?

JULIET   Not proud you have, but thankful that you have:
                Proud can I never be of what I hate,
                But thankful even for hate that is meant love.

CAPULET   How how, how how, chopt-logic? What is this?
150   'Proud', and 'I thank you', and 'I thank you not',
                   And yet 'not proud', mistress minion you?
                   Thank me no thankings, nor proud me no prouds,
                   But fettle your fine joints 'gainst Thursday next,
                   To go with Paris to Saint Peter's Church,
155   Or I will drag thee on a hurdle thither.
                   Out, you green-sickness carrion! out, you baggage!
                   You tallow-face!

LADY CAPULET   Fie, fie, what, are you mad?

JULIET   Good father, I beseech you on my knees,
                Hear me with patience but to speak a word.

She kneels down

- -

129 conduit fountain

131 counterfeits imitates

131 bark boat

141 take me with you help me to understand

142 How, will she none? what do you mean, she's not interested

145 bride bridegroom

148 that is meant love that is given out of love

149 chopt-logic false argument

151 mistress minion impertinent girl

153 fettle your ... next prepare yourself for next Thursday

155 hurdle A pallet used to drag criminals to the gallows.

156 green-sickness carrion anemic corpse

160 CAPULET Hang thee, young baggage, disobedient wretch!
I tell thee what: get thee to church a'Thursday,
Or never after look me in the face.
Speak not, reply not, do not answer me!
My fingers itch. Wife, we scarce thought us blest
165 That God had lent us but this only child,
But now I see this one is one too much,
And that we have a curse in having her.
Out on her, hilding!

NURSE   God in heaven bless her!
You are to blame, my lord, to rate her so.

170 CAPULET And why, my Lady Wisdom? Hold your tongue,
Good Prudence, smatter with your gossips, go.

NURSE I speak no treason.

CAPULET   O God-i-goden!

NURSE May not one speak?

CAPULET   Peace, you mumbling fool!
Utter your gravity o'er a gossip's bowl,
175 For here we need it not.

LADY CAPULET   You are too hot.

CAPULET God's bread, it makes me mad! Day, night, work, play,
Alone, in company, still my care hath been
To have her match'd; and having now provided
A gentleman of noble parentage,
180 Of fair demesnes, youthful and nobly lign'd,
Stuff'd, as they say, with honourable parts,
Proportion'd as one's thought would wish a man,
And then to have a wretched puling fool,
A whining mammet, in her fortune's tender,
185 To answer 'I'll not wed, I cannot love;
I am too young, I pray you pardon me.'
But and you will not wed, I'll pardon you:
Graze where you will, you shall not house with me.
Look to't, think on't, I do not use to jest.
190 Thursday is near, lay hand on heart, advise:
And you be mine, I'll give you to my friend;
And you be not, hang, beg, starve, die in the streets,
For by my soul, I'll ne'er acknowledge thee,
Nor what is mine shall never do thee good.
195 Trust to't, bethink you, I'll not be forsworn.   [Exit

168 **hilding** hussy; wench
169 **rate** berate; insult
171 **smatter with your gossips** chat with your old-women friends
172 **God-i-goden** good night (for heaven's sake)
174 **gravity** wisdom
174 **gossip's bowl** drinks with other women
177 **still** always
180 **demesnes** landholdings
180 **nobly lign'd** from a good family
181 **parts** attributes
183 **puling** whining
184 **mammet** puppet
184 **in her fortune's tender** when good luck comes her way
187 **and** if
189 **I do not use to jest** I'm not the type to make jokes
195 **bethink you** think about it
195 **be forsworn** go back on my word

JULIET	Is there no pity sitting in the clouds
	That sees into the bottom of my grief?
	O sweet my mother, cast me not away!
	Delay this marriage for a month, a week,
200	Or if you do not, make the bridal bed
	In that dim monument where Tybalt lies.
LADY CAPULET	Talk not to me, for I'll not speak a word.
	Do as thou wilt, for I have done with thee. [*Exit*
JULIET	O God!—O Nurse, how shall this be prevented?
205	My husband is on earth, my faith in heaven;
	How shall that faith return again to earth,
	Unless that husband send it me from heaven
	By leaving earth? Comfort me, counsel me.
	Alack, alack, that heaven should practise stratagems
210	Upon so soft a subject as myself!
	What say'st thou? hast thou not a word of joy?
	Some comfort, Nurse.
NURSE	Faith, here it is:
	Romeo is banish'd, and all the world to nothing
	That he dares ne'er come back to challenge you;
215	Or if he do, it needs must be by stealth.
	Then since the case so stands as now it doth,
	I think it best you married with the County.
	O, he's a lovely gentleman!
	Romeo's a dishclout to him. An eagle, madam,
220	Hath not so green, so quick, so fair an eye
	As Paris hath. Beshrew my very heart,
	I think you are happy in this second match,
	For it excels your first, or if it did not,
	Your first is dead, or 'twere as good he were
225	As living here and you no use of him.
JULIET	Speak'st thou from thy heart?
NURSE	And from my soul too, else beshrew them both.
JULIET	Amen.
NURSE	What?
230 JULIET	Well, thou hast comforted me marvellous much.
	Go in, and tell my lady I am gone,
	Having displeas'd my father, to Lawrence' cell,
	To make confession and to be absolv'd.
NURSE	Marry, I will, and this is wisely done. [*Exit*

· ·

203 have done with thee have had
it with you
209 practise stratagems play games

213 all the world to nothing I'll bet
you anything
214 challenge you claim you
219 dishclout dishcloth

221 Beshrew my very heart cursed
be my own heart (a mild oath)

235 JULIET   [*She looks after* NURSE] Ancient damnation! O most wicked fiend!
                  Is it more sin to wish me thus forsworn,
                  Or to dispraise my lord with that same tongue
                  Which she hath prais'd him with above compare
                  So many thousand times? Go, counsellor,
240   Thou and my bosom henceforth shall be twain.
                  I'll to the Friar to know his remedy;
                  If all else fail, myself have power to die.   [*Exit*

. . . .

235 Ancient damnation! cursed old   **236 to wish me thus forsworn** to   **240 my bosom** my secret thoughts   **240 twain** separated
woman   suggest I break my marriage vow

ACT 4 Scene 1

Tuesday morning: FRIAR LAWRENCE'*s cell. Enter* FRIAR
LAWRENCE *and* COUNTY PARIS

FRIAR LAWRENCE   On Thursday, sir? the time is very short.

PARIS   My father Capulet will have it so,
And I am nothing slow to slack his haste.

FRIAR LAWRENCE   You say you do not know the lady's mind?

5   Uneven is the course, I like it not.

PARIS   Immoderately she weeps for Tybalt's death,
And therefore have I little talk'd of love,
For Venus smiles not in a house of tears.
Now, sir, her father counts it dangerous

10   That she do give her sorrow so much sway;
And in his wisdom hastes our marriage
To stop the inundation of her tears,
Which too much minded by herself alone
May be put from her by society.

15   Now do you know the reason of this haste.

FRIAR LAWRENCE   [*Aside*] I would I knew not why it should be slow'd.—
Look, sir, here comes the lady toward my cell.

Enter JULIET

PARIS   Happily met, my lady and my wife!

JULIET   That may be, sir, when I may be a wife.

20   PARIS   That 'may be' must be, love, on Thursday next.

JULIET   What must be shall be.

FRIAR LAWRENCE   That's a certain text.

PARIS   Come you to make confession to this father?

JULIET   To answer that, I should confess to you.

PARIS   Do not deny to him that you love me.

25   JULIET   I will confess to you that I love him.

PARIS   So will ye, I am sure, that you love me.

JULIET   If I do so, it will be of more price,
Being spoke behind your back, than to your face.

PARIS   Poor soul, thy face is much abus'd with tears.

30   JULIET   The tears have got small victory by that,
For it was bad enough before their spite.

PARIS   Thou wrong'st it more than tears with that report.

- -

3 nothing slow to slack his haste   not interested in slowing him down

5 Uneven is the course   this is an unusual approach to marriage

8 Venus   Roman goddess of love.

10 sway   influence

12 inundation   flood

13 too much minded by herself alone   preoccupy her too much when she is alone

14 put from her   lessened; taken away

14 society   company

27 more price   more value

32 report   description

JULIET	That is no slander, sir, which is a truth,
	And what I spake, I spake it to my face.

35 PARIS   Thy face is mine, and thou hast slander'd it.

   JULIET   It may be so, for it is not mine own.
            Are you at leisure, holy father, now,
            Or shall I come to you at evening mass?

   FRIAR LAWRENCE   My leisure serves me, pensive daughter, now.
40   My lord, we must entreat the time alone.

   PARIS   God shield I should disturb devotion!
            Juliet, on Thursday early will I rouse ye;
            Till then adieu, and keep this holy kiss.   [*Exit*

   JULIET   O shut the door, and when thou hast done so,
45   Come weep with me, past hope, past cure, past help!

   FRIAR LAWRENCE   O Juliet, I already know thy grief,
            It strains me past the compass of my wits.
            I hear thou must, and nothing may prorogue it,
            On Thursday next be married to this County.

50 JULIET   Tell me not, Friar, that thou hearest of this,
            Unless thou tell me how I may prevent it.
            If in thy wisdom thou canst give no help,
            Do thou but call my resolution wise,
            And with this knife I'll help it presently.
55   God join'd my heart and Romeo's, thou our hands,
            And ere this hand, by thee to Romeo's seal'd,
            Shall be the label to another deed,
            Or my true heart with treacherous revolt
            Turn to another, this shall slay them both:
60   Therefore, out of thy long-experienc'd time,
            Give me some present counsel, or, behold,
            'Twixt my extremes and me this bloody knife
            Shall play the umpire, arbitrating that
            Which the commission of thy years and art
65   Could to no issue of true honour bring.
            Be not so long to speak, I long to die,
            If what thou speak'st speak not of remedy.

   FRIAR LAWRENCE   Hold, daughter, I do spy a kind of hope,
            Which craves as desperate an execution
70   As that is desperate which we would prevent.
            If, rather than to marry County Paris,
            Thou hast the strength of will to slay thyself,

....

39 pensive thoughtful; sad

40 entreat request

42 rouse wake

47 compass of my wits limits of my imagination

48 prorogue delay

53 Do thou but just

53 resolution decision

54 presently right now

56–57 ere this ... deed before I give my hand, which you connected to Romeo's (in marriage), to someone else

59 both i.e., her heart and her hand

61 present immediate

62 'Twixt my extremes between my desperate circumstances

63–65 arbitrating that ... bring settling the problem that you, with all your experience and skill, couldn't resolve honourably

69–70 craves as ... prevent requires action as desperate as that which we are trying to prevent

                    Then it is likely thou wilt undertake
                    A thing like death to chide away this shame,
75   That cop'st with Death himself to scape from it;
                    And if thou dar'st, I'll give thee remedy.

JULIET   O bid me leap, rather than marry Paris,
                    From off the battlements of any tower,
                    Or walk in thievish ways, or bid me lurk
80   Where serpents are; chain me with roaring bears,
                    Or hide me nightly in a charnel-house,
                    O'ercover'd quite with dead men's rattling bones,
                    With reeky shanks and yellow chapless skulls;
                    Or bid me go into a new-made grave,
85   And hide me with a dead man in his shroud—
                    Things that to hear them told have made me tremble—
                    And I will do it without fear or doubt,
                    To live an unstain'd wife to my sweet love.

FRIAR LAWRENCE Hold then, go home, be merry, give consent
90   To marry Paris. Wednesday is tomorrow;
                    Tomorrow night look that thou lie alone,
                    Let not the Nurse lie with thee in thy chamber.
                    Take thou this vial, being then in bed,
                    And this distilling liquor drink thou off,
95   When presently through all thy veins shall run
                    A cold and drowsy humour; for no pulse
                    Shall keep his native progress, but surcease;
                    No warmth, no breath shall testify thou livest;
                    The roses in thy lips and cheeks shall fade
100   To wanny ashes, thy eyes' windows fall,
                    Like Death when he shuts up the day of life;
                    Each part, depriv'd of supple government,
                    Shall stiff and stark and cold appear like death,
                    And in this borrow'd likeness of shrunk death
105   Thou shalt continue two and forty hours,
                    And then awake as from a pleasant sleep.
                    Now when the bridegroom in the morning comes
                    To rouse thee from thy bed, there art thou dead.
                    Then as the manner of our country is,
110   In thy best robes, uncover'd on the bier,
                    Thou shall be borne to that same ancient vault
                    Where all the kindred of the Capulets lie.
                    In the mean time, against thou shalt awake,

74 chide away drive away

75 cop'st with grapples with

75 scape escape

79 thievish ways places where thieves operate

81 charnel-house A place where bones dug up in a graveyard were kept.

83 reeky shanks putrid limbs

83 chapless jawless

93 vial small glass bottle

96 humour fluid

96–97 no pulse … progress you will have no pulse

97 surcease stop

100 wanny wan; pale

102 government control of movement

113 against thou before

115 Shall Romeo by my letters know our drift,
And hither shall he come, and he and I
Will watch thy waking, and that very night
Shall Romeo bear thee hence to Mantua.
And this shall free thee from this present shame,
If no inconstant toy, nor womanish fear,
120 Abate thy valour in the acting it.

JULIET   Give me, give me! O tell not me of fear.

FRIAR LAWRENCE Hold, get you gone, be strong and prosperous
In this resolve; I'll send a friar with speed
To Mantua, with my letters to thy lord.

125 JULIET   Love give me strength, and strength shall help afford.
Farewell, dear father.   [*Exeunt*

Scene 2

Tuesday afternoon: CAPULET's *house. Enter father,*
CAPULET, *mother,* LADY CAPULET, NURSE *and*
SERVINGMEN, *two or three*

CAPULET   So many guests invite as here are writ.   [*Exit* SERVINGMAN
Sirrah, go hire me twenty cunning cooks.

SERVINGMAN   You shall have none ill, sir, for I'll try if they can lick
their fingers.

5 CAPULET   How canst thou try them so?

SERVINGMAN   Marry, sir, 'tis an ill cook that cannot lick his own
fingers; therefore he that cannot lick his fingers goes not
with me.

CAPULET   Go, be gone.   [*Exit* SERVINGMAN
10 We shall be much unfurnish'd for this time.
What, is my daughter gone to Friar Lawrence?

NURSE   Ay forsooth.

CAPULET   Well, he may chance to do some good on her.
A peevish self-will'd harlotry it is.

Enter JULIET

15 NURSE   See where she comes from shrift with merry look.

CAPULET   How now, my headstrong, where have you been gadding?

. . . .

114 drift thinking; plan

119 inconstant toy passing whim

125 help afford aid me

2 Sirrah A title used when
addressing those of lower rank.

2 cunning skillful

3 none ill no bad cooks

3 try if check if

10 unfurnish'd unprepared

12 forsooth in truth; indeed

13 do some good on her do her
some good

14 harlotry brat

15 shrift confession

16 headstrong stubborn one

16 gadding wandering

JULIET	Where I have learnt me to repent the sin
	Of disobedient opposition
	To you and your behests, and am enjoin'd
20	By holy Lawrence to fall prostrate here
	To beg your pardon.

She kneels down

	Pardon, I beseech you!
	Henceforward I am ever rul'd by you.
CAPULET	Send for the County, go tell him of this.
	I'll have this knot knit up tomorrow morning.
25 JULIET	I met the youthful lord at Lawrence' cell,
	And gave him what becomed love I might,
	Not stepping o'er the bounds of modesty.
CAPULET	Why, I am glad on't, this is well, stand up.
	This is as't should be. Let me see the County;
30	Ay, marry, go, I say, and fetch him hither.
	Now afore God, this reverend holy Friar,
	All our whole city is much bound to him.
JULIET	Nurse, will you go with me into my closet,
	To help me sort such needful ornaments
35	As you think fit to furnish me tomorrow?
LADY CAPULET	No, not till Thursday, there is time enough.
CAPULET	Go, Nurse, go with her, we'll to church tomorrow.

[*Exeunt* JULIET *and* NURSE

LADY CAPULET	We shall be short in our provision,
	'Tis now near night.
CAPULET	Tush, I will stir about,
40	And all things shall be well, I warrant thee, wife:
	Go thou to Juliet, help to deck up her;
	I'll not to bed tonight; let me alone,
	I'll play the huswife for this once. What ho!
	They are all forth. Well, I will walk myself
45	To County Paris, to prepare up him
	Against tomorrow. My heart is wondrous light,
	Since this same wayward girl is so reclaim'd. [*Exeunt*

---

19 behests wishes

19 enjoin'd directed

20 prostrate flat

22 ever always

24 this knot knit up this match made

26 becomed becoming; appropriate

33 closet private chambers

34 needful ornaments required clothes

38 We shall be short in our provision we won't have enough food and drink

43 huswife housewife

44 forth out

46 Against for

Scene 3

Tuesday night: JULIET's *bedroom. Enter* JULIET *and* NURSE

JULIET Ay, those attires are best, but, gentle Nurse,
    I pray thee leave me to myself tonight:
    For I have need of many orisons
    To move the heavens to smile upon my state,
5   Which, well thou knowest, is cross and full of sin.

Enter mother, LADY CAPULET

LADY CAPULET What, are you busy, ho? need you my help?

JULIET No, madam, we have cull'd such necessaries
    As are behoveful for our state tomorrow.
    So please you, let me now be left alone,
10   And let the Nurse this night sit up with you,
    For I am sure you have your hands full all,
    In this so sudden business.

LADY CAPULET   Good night.
    Get thee to bed and rest, for thou hast need.

        [*Exeunt* LADY CAPULET *and* NURSE

JULIET Farewell! God knows when we shall meet again.
15   I have a faint cold fear thrills through my veins
    That almost freezes up the heat of life:
    I'll call them back again to comfort me.
    Nurse!—What should she do here?
    My dismal scene I needs must act alone.
20   Come, vial.
    What if this mixture do not work at all?
    Shall I be married then tomorrow morning?
    No, no, this shall forbid it; lie thou there.

Laying down her dagger

    What if it be a poison which the Friar
25   Subtly hath minister'd to have me dead,
    Lest in this marriage he should be dishonour'd,
    Because he married me before to Romeo?
    I fear it is, and yet methinks it should not,
    For he hath still been tried a holy man.
30   How if, when I am laid into the tomb,
    I wake before the time that Romeo

---

1 attires clothes

3 orisons prayers

5 cross rebellious

7 cull'd selected

8 behoveful appropriate

25 Subtly deviously

25 minister'd administered; prescribed

29 still always

29 tried proved

Come to redeem me? There's a fearful point!
Shall I not then be stifl'd in the vault,
To whose foul mouth no healthsome air breathes in,
35 And there die strangl'd ere my Romeo comes?
Or if I live, is it not very like
The horrible conceit of death and night,
Together with the terror of the place—
As in a vault, an ancient receptacle,
40 Where for this many hundred years the bones
Of all my buried ancestors are pack'd,
Where bloody Tybalt, yet but green in earth,
Lies fest'ring in his shroud, where, as they say,
At some hours in the night spirits resort—
45 Alack, alack, is it not like that I,
So early waking—what with loathsome smells,
And shrieks like mandrakes' torn out of the earth,
That living mortals hearing them run mad—
O, if I wake, shall I not be distraught,
50 Environed with all these hideous fears,
And madly play with my forefathers' joints,
And pluck the mangl'd Tybalt from his shroud,
And in this rage, with some great kinsman's bone,
As with a club, dash out my desp'rate brains?
55 O look! methinks I see my cousin's ghost
Seeking out Romeo that did spit his body
Upon a rapier's point. Stay, Tybalt, stay!
Romeo, Romeo, Romeo! Here's drink—I drink to thee.

She falls upon her bed, within the curtains

Scene 4

Early Wednesday morning: CAPULET's *house. Enter
lady of the house,* LADY CAPULET *and* NURSE *with
herbs*

LADY CAPULET   Hold, take these keys and fetch more spices, Nurse.

NURSE   They call for dates and quinces in the pastry.

Enter old CAPULET

CAPULET   Come, stir, stir, stir! the second cock hath crow'd,
The curfew bell hath rung, 'tis three a'clock.
5 Look to the bak'd meats, good Angelica,

---

32 redeem save

36 like likely

37 conceit thought; mental image

39 As being

42 green in earth recently laid to rest

47 mandrakes A type of plant that was said to shriek when pulled from the earth, and to cause death or madness.

50 Environed surrounded

53 rage madness

56 spit skewer

2 pastry section of the kitchen where pies were prepared

5 bak'd meats meat pies and other pastries

5 Angelica Perhaps this is the Nurse's first name.

Spare not for cost.

NURSE   Go, you cot-quean, go,
Get you to bed. Faith, you'll be sick tomorrow
For this night's watching.

CAPULET   No, not a whit. What, I have watch'd ere now
10   All night for lesser cause, and ne'er been sick.

LADY CAPULET   Ay, you have been a mouse-hunt in your time,
But I will watch you from such watching now.

[Exeunt LADY CAPULET *and* NURSE

CAPULET   A jealous-hood, a jealous-hood!

Enter three or four SERVINGMEN *with spits and logs
and baskets*

Now, fellow,
What is there?

15 FIRST SERVINGMAN   Things for the cook, sir, but I know not what.

CAPULET   Make haste, make haste.   *[Exit* FIRST SERVINGMAN
Sirrah, fetch drier logs.
Call Peter, he will show thee where they are.

SECOND SERVINGMAN   I have a head, sir, that will find out logs,
And never trouble Peter for the matter.

20 CAPULET   Mass, and well said, a merry whoreson, ha!
Thou shalt be loggerhead.

[Exeunt SECOND SERVINGMAN *and any others*

Good faith, 'tis day.
The County will be here with music straight,
For so he said he would.

Play music within

I hear him near.
Nurse! Wife! What ho! What, Nurse, I say!

Enter NURSE

25   Go waken Juliet, go and trim her up,
I'll go and chat with Paris. Hie, make haste,
Make haste, the bridegroom he is come already,
Make haste, I say.   *[Exit*

6 Spare not for cost spare no expense

6 cot-quean man who does housework

9 not a whit not in the least

11 mouse-hunt skirt-chaser

12 watch you from such watching prevent you from that kind of late-night activity

13 jealous-hood jealousy

20 Mass by the Mass (a mild oath)

21 loggerhead blockhead; the person in charge of getting firewood

22 straight any minute; straightaway

25 trim her up get her ready

Scene 5

JULIET's *bedroom*

NURSE   Mistress, what mistress! Juliet! Fast, I warrant her, she.
Why, lamb! why, lady! fie, you slug-a-bed!
Why, love, I say! madam! sweet heart! why, bride!
What, not a word? You take your pennyworths now;

5   Sleep for a week, for the next night I warrant
The County Paris hath set up his rest
That you shall rest but little. God forgive me!
Marry and amen! How sound is she asleep!
I needs must wake her. Madam, madam, madam!

10   Ay, let the County take you in your bed,
He'll fright you up, i'faith. Will it not be?

Draws back the curtains

What, dress'd, and in your clothes, and down again?
I must needs wake you. Lady, lady, lady!
Alas, alas! Help, help! my lady's dead!

15   O weraday that ever I was born!
Some aqua-vitae, ho! My lord! My lady!

Enter mother, LADY CAPULET

LADY CAPULET   What noise is here?

NURSE   O lamentable day!

LADY CAPULET   What is the matter?

NURSE   Look, look! O heavy day!

LADY CAPULET   O me, O me, my child, my only life!

20   Revive, look up, or I will die with thee.
Help, help! Call help.

Enter father, CAPULET

CAPULET   For shame, bring Juliet forth, her lord is come.

NURSE   She's dead, deceas'd, she's dead, alack the day!

LADY CAPULET   Alack the day, she's dead, she's dead, she's dead!

25 CAPULET   Hah, let me see her. Out alas, she's cold,
Her blood is settled, and her joints are stiff:
Life and these lips have long been separated;
Death lies on her like an untimely frost
Upon the sweetest flower of all the field.

---

1 Fast fast asleep
2 slug-a-bed lazybones

4 take your pennyworths get
whatever sleep you can
6 set up his rest determined

10 take discover
15 weraday alas

16 aqua-vitae brandy
26 settled stopped flowing

30 NURSE   O lamentable day!

    LADY CAPULET   O woeful time!

    CAPULET   Death that hath tane her hence to make me wail
                   Ties up my tongue and will not let me speak.

Enter FRIAR LAWRENCE *and the* COUNTY PARIS *with the* MUSICIANS

    FRIAR LAWRENCE   Come, is the bride ready to go to church?

    CAPULET   Ready to go, but never to return.—
35   O son, the night before thy wedding day
                   Hath Death lain with thy wife. There she lies,
                   Flower as she was, deflowered by him.
                   Death is my son-in-law, Death is my heir,
                   My daughter he hath wedded. I will die,
40   And leave him all; life, living, all is Death's.

    PARIS   Have I thought long to see this morning's face,
                   And doth it give me such a sight as this?

    LADY CAPULET Accurs'd, unhappy, wretched, hateful day!
                   Most miserable hour that e'er time saw
45   In lasting labour of his pilgrimage!
                   But one, poor one, one poor and loving child,
                   But one thing to rejoice and solace in,
                   And cruel Death hath catch'd it from my sight!

    NURSE   O woe! O woeful, woeful, woeful day!
50   Most lamentable day, most woeful day
                   That ever, ever, I did yet behold!
                   O day, O day, O day, O hateful day!
                   Never was seen so black a day as this.
                   O woeful day, O woeful day!

55 PARIS   Beguil'd, divorced, wronged, spited, slain!
                   Most detestable Death, by thee beguil'd,
                   By cruel, cruel thee quite overthrown!
                   O love! O life! not life, but love in death!

    CAPULET   Despis'd, distressed, hated, martyr'd, kill'd!
60   Uncomfortable time, why cam'st thou now
                   To murder, murder our solemnity?
                   O child, O child! my soul, and not my child!
                   Dead art thou. Alack, my child is dead,
                   And with my child my joys are buried.

65 FRIAR LAWRENCE Peace ho, for shame! Confusion's cure lives not
                   In these confusions. Heaven and yourself

---

37 deflowered   ravaged

45 In lasting labour of his pilgrimage
in all his everlasting journey

55 Beguil'd   cheated

57 overthrown   ruined

61 solemnity   wedding ceremony

65–66 Confusion's cure ... confusions.
these distressed laments are not the
way to cure distress

Had part in this fair maid, now heaven hath all,

And all the better is it for the maid:

Your part in her you could not keep from death,

70   But heaven keeps his part in eternal life.

The most you sought was her promotion,

For 'twas your heaven she should be advanc'd,

And weep ye now, seeing she is advanc'd

Above the clouds, as high as heaven itself?

75   O, in this love, you love your child so ill

That you run mad, seeing that she is well.

She's not well married that lives married long,

But she's best married that dies married young.

Dry up your tears, and stick your rosemary

80   On this fair corse, and as the custom is,

And in her best array, bear her to church;

For though fond nature bids us all lament,

Yet nature's tears are reason's merriment.

CAPULET   All things that we ordained festival,

85   Turn from their office to black funeral:

Our instruments to melancholy bells,

Our wedding cheer to sad burial feast;

Our solemn hymns to sullen dirges change;

Our bridal flowers serve for a buried corse;

90   And all things change them to the contrary.

FRIAR LAWRENCE   Sir, go you in, and, madam, go with him,

And go, Sir Paris. Every one prepare

To follow this fair corse unto her grave.

The heavens do low'r upon you for some ill;

95   Move them no more by crossing their high will.

They all, but the NURSE *and the* MUSICIANS, *go forth,*
casting rosemary on her, and shutting the curtains

FIRST MUSICIAN   Faith, we may put up our pipes and be gone.

NURSE   Honest good fellows, ah put up, put up,

For well you know this is a pitiful case.   [*Exit*

FIRST MUSICIAN   Ay, by my troth, the case may be amended.

Enter PETER

100 PETER   Musicians, O musicians, 'Heart's ease', 'Heart's ease'! O,

and you will have me live, play 'Heart's ease'.

FIRST MUSICIAN   Why 'Heart's ease'?

---

67 Had part in   shared

69 Your part in her   Juliet's earthly body

70 his part   Juliet's soul

71 promotion   social advancement

72 your heaven   your highest wish

77–78 She's not … young.   it's better to die while love is in full bloom; the best marriages are short ones

79 rosemary   A herb used at both weddings and funerals as a symbol of remembrance.

82 fond   foolish

83 nature's tears … merriment   reason laughs at our silly tears (because it knows Juliet is in a better place)

84 festival   festive; for celebration

85 office   intended purpose

87 cheer   food

88 sullen dirges   sad funeral hymns

94 low'r   frown

95 Move   upset

96 put up   pack up

99 amended   mended (he thinks the Nurse is referring to his instrument case)

PETER   O musicians, because my heart itself plays 'My heart is
full'. O play me some merry dump to comfort me.

105 MUSICIANS   Not a dump we, 'tis no time to play now.

PETER   You will not then?

FIRST MUSICIAN   No.

PETER   I will then give it you soundly.

FIRST MUSICIAN   What will you give us?

110 PETER   No money, on my faith, but the gleek; I will give you the
minstrel.

FIRST MUSICIAN   Then will I give you the serving-creature.

PETER   Then will I lay the serving-creature's dagger on your
pate. I will carry no crotchets, I'll re you, I'll fa you. Do
115   you note me?

FIRST MUSICIAN   And you re us and fa us, you note us.

SECOND MUSICIAN   Pray you put up your dagger, and put out your wit.

PETER   Then have at you with my wit! I will dry-beat you with
an iron wit, and put up my iron dagger. Answer me like
120   men:
         'When griping griefs the heart doth wound,
         And doleful dumps the mind oppress,
         Then music with her silver sound—'
Why 'silver sound'? why 'music with her silver sound'?
125   What say you Simon Catling?

FIRST MUSICIAN   Marry, sir, because silver hath a sweet sound.

PETER   Prates! What say you, Hugh Rebeck?

SECOND MUSICIAN   I say 'silver sound' because musicians sound for silver.

PETER   Prates too! What say you, James Soundpost?

130 THIRD MUSICIAN   Faith, I know not what to say.

PETER   O, I cry you mercy, you are the singer; I will say for you:
It is 'music with her silver sound' because musicians
have no gold for sounding.
         'Then music with her silver sound
135   With speedy help doth lend redress.'   [Exit

FIRST MUSICIAN   What a pestilent knave is this same!

SECOND MUSICIAN   Hang him, Jack! Come, we'll in here, tarry for the
mourners, and stay dinner.   [Exeunt

104 dump sad song

108 give it you soundly beat you thoroughly (with a pun on "sound")

110 the gleek "Give you the gleek" meant "mock you."

110-111 give you the minstrel An insult because minstrels were looked down upon.

114 pate head

114 I will carry no crotchets I won't put up with your crazy ideas (crotchets: musical notes)

114 I'll re you, I'll fa you I'll beat you (re, fa: musical notes)

117 put out your wit use your good sense

125 Catling fiddle string

127 Prates! nonsense

127 Rebeck A type of fiddle.

128 sound for silver play for money

129 Soundpost A small wooden post inside most stringed instruments.

133 have no gold for sounding make little money for playing ("sounding")

135 lend redress offer comfort

137 tarry wait

138 stay dinner await dinner

ACT 5 Scene 1

Wednesday morning: Mantua. Enter ROMEO

ROMEO If I may trust the flattering truth of sleep,
  My dreams presage some joyful news at hand.
  My bosom's lord sits lightly in his throne,
  And all this day an unaccustom'd spirit
5 Lifts me above the ground with cheerful thoughts.
  I dreamt my lady came and found me dead
  (Strange dream that gives a dead man leave to think!),
  And breath'd such life with kisses in my lips
  That I reviv'd and was an emperor.
10 Ah me, how sweet is love itself possess'd,
  When but love's shadows are so rich in joy!

Enter ROMEO*'s man* BALTHASAR, *booted*

  News from Verona! How now, Balthasar?
  Dost thou not bring me letters from the Friar?
  How doth my lady! Is my father well?
15 How doth my Juliet? That I ask again,
  For nothing can be ill if she be well.

BALTHASAR Then she is well and nothing can be ill:
  Her body sleeps in Capels' monument,
  And her immortal part with angels lives.
20 I saw her laid low in her kindred's vault,
  And presently took post to tell it you.
  O pardon me for bringing these ill news,
  Since you did leave it for my office, sir.

ROMEO Is it e'en so? then I defy you, stars!
25 Thou knowest my lodging, get me ink and paper,
  And hire post-horses; I will hence tonight.

BALTHASAR I do beseech you, sir, have patience:
  Your looks are pale and wild, and do import
  Some misadventure.

ROMEO   Tush, thou art deceiv'd.
30 Leave me, and do the thing I bid thee do.
  Hast thou no letters to me from the Friar?

BALTHASAR No, my good lord.

ROMEO   No matter, get thee gone,
  And hire those horses; I'll be with thee straight. [*Exit* BALTHASAR

---

1 flattering truth wishful thinking

2 presage predict

3 My bosom's...throne my heart is light

7 gives a deadman leave allows a dead man

11 love's shadows illusions of love

11 s.d. booted wearing riding boots

18 Capel's monument the Capulet tomb

19 immortal part soul

21 took post rode quickly

23 for my office as my duty

24 Is it e'en so? is that so

28–29 import / Some misadventure suggest something bad will happen

Well, Juliet, I will lie with thee tonight.

35   Let's see for means. O mischief, thou art swift

To enter in the thoughts of desperate men!

I do remember an apothecary,

And hereabouts 'a dwells, which late I noted

In tatter'd weeds, with overwhelming brows,

40   Culling of simples; meagre were his looks,

Sharp misery had worn him to the bones;

And in his needy shop a tortoise hung,

An alligator stuff'd, and other skins

Of ill-shap'd fishes, and about his shelves

45   A beggarly account of empty boxes,

Green earthen pots, bladders, and musty seeds,

Remnants of packthread, and old cakes of roses

Were thinly scatter'd, to make up a show.

Noting this penury, to myself I said,

50   'And if a man did need a poison now,

Whose sale is present death in Mantua,

Here lives a caitiff wretch would sell it him.'

O this same thought did but forerun my need,

And this same needy man must sell it me.

55   As I remember, this should be the house.

Being holiday, the beggar's shop is shut.

What ho, apothecary!

Enter APOTHECARY

APOTHECARY   Who calls so loud?

ROMEO   Come hither, man. I see that thou art poor.

Hold, there is forty ducats; let me have

60   A dram of poison, such soon-speeding gear

As will disperse itself through all the veins,

That the life-weary taker may fall dead,

And that the trunk may be discharg'd of breath

As violently as hasty powder fir'd

65   Doth hurry from the fatal cannon's womb.

APOTHECARY   Such mortal drugs I have, but Mantua's law

Is death to any he that utters them.

ROMEO   Art thou so bare and full of wretchedness,

And fearest to die? Famine is in thy cheeks,

70   Need and oppression starveth in thy eyes,

Contempt and beggary hangs upon thy back;

. . . .

35 Let's see for means. let me think how I will go about it

39 weeds clothes

39 overwhelming overhanging

40 Culling of simples collecting herbs to make medicines

45 beggarly account pathetic collection

46 bladders animal skin pouches for holding liquid (or possibly actual bladders)

47 packthread string

47 cakes of roses perfume made from pressed rose petals

51 present death punishable by immediate execution

52 caitiff pitiful

59 ducats gold coins

60 soon-speeding fast-acting

63 trunk body

64 powder fir'd gunpowder set alight

67 utters sells

70 Need and ... eyes your hungry look tells of need and hardship

71 hangs upon thy back shows in how you are dressed

The world is not thy friend, nor the world's law,

The world affords no law to make thee rich;

Then be not poor, but break it and take this.

75 APOTHECARY   My poverty, but not my will, consents.

ROMEO   I pay thy poverty and not thy will.

APOTHECARY   Put this in any liquid thing you will

And drink it off, and if you had the strength

Of twenty men, it would dispatch you straight.

80 ROMEO   There is thy gold, worse poison to men's souls,

Doing more murder in this loathsome world,

Than these poor compounds that thou mayst not sell.

I sell thee poison, thou hast sold me none.

Farewell, buy food, and get thyself in flesh.   [*Exit* APOTHECARY

85   Come, cordial and not poison, go with me

To Juliet's grave, for there must I use thee.   [*Exit*

Scene 2

Verona: FRIAR LAWRENCE*'s cell. Enter* FRIAR JOHN

FRIAR JOHN   Holy Franciscan friar, brother, ho!

Enter FRIAR LAWRENCE

FRIAR LAWRENCE   This same should be the voice of Friar John.

Welcome from Mantua. What says Romeo?

Or if his mind be writ, give me his letter.

5   FRIAR JOHN Going to find a barefoot brother out,

One of our order, to associate me,

Here in this city visiting the sick,

And finding him, the searchers of the town,

Suspecting that we both were in a house

10   Where the infectious pestilence did reign,

Seal'd up the doors, and would not let us forth,

So that my speed to Mantua there was stay'd.

FRIAR LAWRENCE   Who bare my letter then to Romeo?

FRIAR JOHN I could not send it—here it is again—

15   Nor get a messenger to bring it thee,

So fearful were they of infection.

FRIAR LAWRENCE   Unhappy fortune! By my brotherhood,

The letter was not nice but full of charge,

Of dear import, and the neglecting it

....

73 affords   provides

74 break it   break the law

79 dispatch you straight   kill you immediately

84 get thyself in flesh   fatten yourself up

85 cordial   reviving drink

4 if his mind be writ   if he has written down his thoughts

5 a barefoot brother   another Franciscan

6 to associate me   to accompany me

8 searchers   Inspectors who checked bodies for signs of the plague.

10 the infectious pestilence   the plague

13 bare   delivered

18 nice   trivial

18 full of charge   contained very serious matters

19 dear import   great importance

20   May do much danger. Friar John, go hence,
                     Get me an iron crow and bring it straight
                     Unto my cell.

FRIAR JOHN Brother, I'll go and bring it thee.   [*Exit*

FRIAR LAWRENCE   Now must I to the monument alone,

25   Within this three hours will fair Juliet wake.
                     She will beshrew me much that Romeo
                     Hath had no notice of these accidents;
                     But I will write again to Mantua,
                     And keep her at my cell till Romeo come,

30   Poor living corse, clos'd in a dead man's tomb!   [*Exit*

Scene 3

Verona: a churchyard, with the tomb of the CAPULETS.
Enter PARIS *and his* PAGE *with flowers and sweet water
and torch*

PARIS   Give me thy torch, boy. Hence, and stand aloof.
                     Yet put it out, for I would not be seen.
                     Under yond yew trees lay thee all along,
                     Holding thy ear close to the hollow ground,

5   So shall no foot upon the churchyard tread,
                     Being loose, unfirm with digging up of graves,
                     But thou shalt hear it. Whistle then to me
                     As signal that thou hear'st something approach.
                     Give me those flowers. Do as I bid thee, go.

10 PAGE   [*Aside*] I am almost afraid to stand alone
                     Here in the churchyard, yet I will adventure.   [*Retires*

PARIS *strews the tomb with flowers*

PARIS   Sweet flower, with flowers thy bridal bed I strew—
                     O woe, thy canopy is dust and stones!—
                     Which with sweet water nightly I will dew,

15   Or wanting that, with tears distill'd by moans.
                     The obsequies that I for thee will keep
                     Nightly shall be to strew thy grave and weep.

Whistle BOY

                     The boy gives warning, something doth approach.
                     What cursed foot wanders this way tonight,

---

21 iron crow crowbar

26 beshrew curse

27 accidents events

30 corse dead body

0 s.d. sweet water perfumed water

1 aloof at a distance

2 would not don't want to

3 all along on the ground

11 adventure take the risk

13 canopy Fabric covering over a bed.

14 dew sprinkle

15 wanting that if I don't have any

16 obsequies death rites

20   To cross my obsequies and true love's rite?
        What, with a torch? Muffle me, night, a while.   [*Retires*

        Enter ROMEO *and* BALTHASAR *with a torch, a mattock,*
        and a crow of iron

ROMEO   Give me that mattock and the wrenching iron.
        Hold, take this letter; early in the morning
        See thou deliver it to my lord and father.
25   Give me the light. Upon thy life I charge thee,
        What e'er thou hear'st or seest, stand all aloof,
        And do not interrupt me in my course.
        Why I descend into this bed of death
        Is partly to behold my lady's face,
30   But chiefly to take thence from her dead finger
        A precious ring, a ring that I must use
        In dear employment; therefore hence, be gone.
        But if thou, jealous, dost return to pry
        In what I farther shall intend to do,
35   By heaven, I will tear thee joint by joint,
        And strew this hungry churchyard with thy limbs.
        The time and my intents are savage-wild,
        More fierce and more inexorable far
        Than empty tigers or the roaring sea.

40 BALTHASAR   I will be gone, sir, and not trouble ye.

ROMEO   So shalt thou show me friendship. Take thou that,

        Gives a purse

        Live and be prosperous, and farewell, good fellow.

BALTHASAR [*Aside*] For all this same, I'll hide me hereabout,
        His looks I fear, and his intents I doubt.   [*Retires*

45 ROMEO   Thou detestable maw, thou womb of death,
        Gorg'd with the dearest morsel of the earth,
        Thus I enforce thy rotten jaws to open,
        And in despite I'll cram thee with more food.

        ROMEO *begins to open the tomb*

PARIS   This is that banish'd haughty Montague,
50   That murder'd my love's cousin, with which grief
        It is supposed the fair creature died,
        And here is come to do some villainous shame
        To the dead bodies. I will apprehend him.

. . . .

20 cross frustrate; interrupt

21 Muffle me hide me

21 s.d. mattock pickaxe

22 wrenching iron crowbar

25 charge order

26 all aloof far back

32 dear employment important business

33 jealous suspicious

38 inexorable unstoppable

39 empty hungry

43 For all this same even so

45 maw mouth; stomach

46 Gorg'd stuffed

48 in despite ... food in defiance, I'll stuff you with more bodies (i.e., his own)

51 the fair creature Juliet

53 apprehend arrest

Steps forth

              Stop thy unhallow'd toil, vile Montague!

55   Can vengeance be pursu'd further than death?
              Condemned villain, I do apprehend thee.
              Obey and go with me, for thou must die.

ROMEO   I must indeed, and therefore came I hither.
              Good gentle youth, tempt not a desp'rate man,

60   Fly hence and leave me. Think upon these gone,
              Let them affright thee. I beseech thee, youth,
              Put not another sin upon my head,
              By urging me to fury: O be gone!
              By heaven, I love thee better than myself,

65   For I come hither arm'd against myself.
              Stay not, be gone; live, and hereafter say,
              A madman's mercy bid thee run away.

PARIS   I do defy thy conjuration,
              And apprehend thee for a felon here.

70 **ROMEO**   Wilt thou provoke me? then have at thee, boy!

They fight

PAGE   O Lord, they fight! I will go call the Watch.   [*Exit*

PARIS   O, I am slain! [*Falls*] If thou be merciful,
              Open the tomb, lay me with Juliet. [*Dies*]

ROMEO   In faith, I will. Let me peruse this face.

75   Mercutio's kinsman, noble County Paris!
              What said my man, when my betossed soul
              Did not attend him as we rode? I think
              He told me Paris should have married Juliet.
              Said he not so? or did I dream it so?

80   Or am I mad, hearing him talk of Juliet,
               To think it was so? O give me thy hand,
              One writ with me in sour misfortune's book!
              I'll bury thee in a triumphant grave.
              A grave? O no, a lantern, slaughter'd youth;

85   For here lies Juliet, and her beauty makes
               This vault a feasting presence full of light.
              Death, lie thou there, by a dead man interr'd.

Laying PARIS *in the tomb*

---

54 unhallow'd unholy

60 these gone the dead bodies in this churchyard

61 affright scare

68 defy thy conjuration reject your appeals

69 for a felon as a criminal

74 peruse examine

76 betossed troubled

78 should have was supposed to have

82 writ with … book who shares my unhappy fate

83 triumphant magnificent

84 lantern A room, often a turret, on the top of a dome or building.

86 feasting presence royal reception hall

How oft when men are at the point of death
Have they been merry, which their keepers call
90 A light'ning before death! O how may I
Call this a light'ning? O my love, my wife,
Death, that hath suck'd the honey of thy breath,
Hath had no power yet upon thy beauty:
Thou art not conquer'd, beauty's ensign yet
95 Is crimson in thy lips and in thy cheeks,
And death's pale flag is not advanced there.
Tybalt, liest thou there in thy bloody sheet?
O, what more favour can I do to thee
Than with that hand that cut thy youth in twain
100 To sunder his that was thine enemy?
Forgive me, cousin. Ah, dear Juliet,
Why art thou yet so fair? Shall I believe
That unsubstantial Death is amorous,
And that the lean abhorred monster keeps
105 Thee here in dark to be his paramour?
For fear of that, I still will stay with thee,
And never from this palace of dim night
Depart again. Here, here will I remain
With worms that are thy chambermaids; O here
110 Will I set up my everlasting rest,
And shake the yoke of inauspicious stars
From this world-wearied flesh. Eyes, look your last!
Arms, take your last embrace! and, lips, O you
The doors of breath, seal with a righteous kiss
115 A dateless bargain to engrossing Death!
Come, bitter conduct, come, unsavoury guide!
Thou desperate pilot, now at once run on
The dashing rocks thy seasick weary bark!
Here's to my love! [*Drinks*] O true apothecary!
120 Thy drugs are quick. Thus with a kiss I die. [*Dies*]

Enter FRIAR LAWRENCE *with lantern, crow, and spade*

FRIAR LAWRENCE   Saint Francis be my speed! how oft tonight
Have my old feet stumbl'd at graves! Who's there?

BALTHASAR Here's one, a friend, and one that knows you well.

FRIAR LAWRENCE   Bliss be upon you! Tell me, good my friend,
125 What torch is yond that vainly lends his light

89 **keepers** attendants
90 **light'ning** brightening; cheering
94 **ensign** flag
100 **sunder his ... enemy** cut short the life of your enemy (i.e., Romeo himself)
103 **unsubstantial** i.e., having no physical body
103 **amorous** in love
105 **paramour** lover
110 **set up my everlasting rest** commit myself once and for all
111 **shake the...stars** free myself from my unlucky fate
115 **dateless bargain** eternal contract
115 **engrossing** all-consuming
116 **conduct** guide; conductor
118 **bark** boat
121 **be my speed** make me quick
122 **stumbl'd at graves** Stumbling on a grave was considered bad luck.

To grubs and eyeless skulls? As I discern,
It burneth in the Capels' monument.

BALTHASAR It doth so, holy sir, and there's my master,
One that you love.

FRIAR LAWRENCE   Who is it?

BALTHASAR   Romeo.

130 FRIAR LAWRENCE How long hath he been there?

BALTHASAR   Full half an hour.

FRIAR LAWRENCE Go with me to the vault.

BALTHASAR   I dare not, sir.
My master knows not but I am gone hence,
And fearfully did menace me with death
If I did stay to look on his intents.

135 FRIAR LAWRENCE Stay then, I'll go alone. Fear comes upon me.
O, much I fear some ill unthrifty thing.

BALTHASAR As I did sleep under this yew tree here,
I dreamt my master and another fought,
And that my master slew him.   [*Retires*

FRIAR LAWRENCE   Romeo!

FRIAR stoops and looks on the blood and weapons

140   Alack, alack, what blood is this which stains
The stony entrance of this sepulchre?
What mean these masterless and gory swords
To lie discolour'd by this place of peace?

Enters the tomb

Romeo! O, pale! Who else? What, Paris too?
145   And steep'd in blood? Ah, what an unkind hour
Is guilty of this lamentable chance!

JULIET rises

The lady stirs.

JULIET O comfortable Friar, where is my lord?
I do remember well where I should be;
150   And there I am. Where is my Romeo?

Noise within

FRIAR LAWRENCE I hear some noise, lady. Come from that nest
Of death, contagion, and unnatural sleep.

- -

127 Capels' Capulets'

132 knows not but thinks

133 fearfully scarily

136 unthrifty unlucky

141 sepulchre grave

142 masterless and gory abandoned and bloody

143 by beside

146 lamentable chance tragic accident

148 comfortable comforting

A greater power than we can contradict
Hath thwarted our intents. Come, come away.
155　Thy husband in thy bosom there lies dead;
And Paris too. Come, I'll dispose of thee
Among a sisterhood of holy nuns.
Stay not to question, for the Watch is coming.
Come go, good Juliet, I dare no longer stay.　　　　　　　　[Exit

160　JULIET　Go get thee hence, for I will not away.
What's here? a cup clos'd in my true love's hand?
Poison I see hath been his timeless end.
O churl, drunk all, and left no friendly drop
To help me after? I will kiss thy lips,
165　Haply some poison yet doth hang on them,
To make me die with a restorative.
Thy lips are warm.

CAPTAIN OF THE WATCH　[Within] Lead, boy, which way?

JULIET　Yea, noise? Then I'll be brief. O happy dagger,

Taking ROMEO's *dagger*

170　　　This is thy sheath;

Stabs herself

　　　　　　　　there rust, and let me die.

Falls on ROMEO's *body and dies*

Enter PARIS'S BOY *and* WATCH

PAGE　This is the place, there where the torch doth burn.

CAPTAIN OF THE WATCH　The ground is bloody, search about the churchyard.
Go, some of you, whoe'er you find attach.
　　　　　　　　　[Exeunt some of the WATCH

The CAPTAIN *enters the tomb and returns*

　　　Pitiful sight! here lies the County slain,
175　And Juliet bleeding, warm, and newly dead,
Who here hath lain this two days buried.
Go tell the prince, run to the Capulets,
Raise up the Montagues; some others search.
　　　　　　　　　[Exeunt others of the WATCH
We see the ground whereon these woes do lie,
180　But the true ground of all these piteous woes
We cannot without circumstance descry.

• •

156 dispose of thee　find you a home　**163 churl**　brute
162 timeless　untimely　**165 Haply**　perhaps

166 To make me die with a restorative
to kill me with the medicine (a kiss)
that should have restored my life

173 attach　arrest

180 true ground　real reason
181 circumstance　a detailed
account
181 descry　understand

Enter one of the WATCH *with* ROMEO's *man* BALTHASAR

SECOND WATCHMAN   Here's Romeo's man, we found him in the churchyard.

CAPTAIN OF THE WATCH   Hold him in safety till the prince come hither.

Enter FRIAR LAWRENCE *and another* WATCHMAN

THIRD WATCHMAN   Here is a friar that trembles, sighs, and weeps.
185   We took this mattock and this spade from him,
                       As he was coming from this churchyard's side.

CAPTAIN OF THE WATCH   A great suspicion. Stay the friar too.

Enter the PRINCE *with others*

PRINCE   What misadventure is so early up,
              That calls our person from our morning rest?

Enter Capels, CAPULET, LADY CAPULET

190 CAPULET   What should it be that is so shriek'd abroad?

LADY CAPULET   O, the people in the street cry 'Romeo',
              Some 'Juliet', and some 'Paris', and all run
              With open outcry toward our monument.

PRINCE   What fear is this which startles in your ears?

195 CAPTAIN OF THE WATCH   Sovereign, here lies the County Paris slain,
              And Romeo dead, and Juliet, dead before,
              Warm and new kill'd.

PRINCE   Search, seek, and know how this foul murder comes.

CAPTAIN OF THE WATCH   Here is a friar, and slaughter'd Romeo's man,
200   With instruments upon them, fit to open
              These dead men's tombs.

CAPULET *and* LADY CAPULET *enter the tomb*

CAPULET   O heavens! O wife, look how our daughter bleeds!
              This dagger hath mistane, for lo his house
              Is empty on the back of Montague,
205   And it mis-sheathed in my daughter's bosom!

LADY CAPULET   O me, this sight of death is as a bell
              That warns my old age to a sepulchre.

They return from the tomb

Enter MONTAGUE

PRINCE   Come, Montague, for thou art early up
              To see thy son and heir now early down.

· ·

200 instruments tools   **203 mistane** made a mistake   **203 house** sheath   **207 warns** calls

210 MONTAGUE Alas, my liege, my wife is dead tonight;
           Grief of my son's exile hath stopp'd her breath.
           What further woe conspires against mine age?

PRINCE   Look and thou shalt see.

MONTAGUE *enters the tomb and returns*

MONTAGUE O thou untaught! what manners is in this,
215   To press before thy father to a grave?

PRINCE   Seal up the mouth of outrage for a while,
           Till we can clear these ambiguities,
           And know their spring, their head, their true descent,
           And then will I be general of your woes,
220   And lead you even to death. Mean time forbear,
           And let mischance be slave to patience.
           Bring forth the parties of suspicion.

FRIAR LAWRENCE I am the greatest, able to do least,
           Yet most suspected, as the time and place
225   Doth make against me, of this direful murder;
           And here I stand both to impeach and purge
           Myself condemned and myself excus'd.

PRINCE   Then say at once what thou dost know in this.

FRIAR LAWRENCE I will be brief, for my short date of breath
230   Is not so long as is a tedious tale.
           Romeo, there dead, was husband to that Juliet,
           And she, there dead, that Romeo's faithful wife:
           I married them, and their stol'n marriage day
           Was Tybalt's doomsday, whose untimely death
235   Banish'd the new-made bridegroom from this city,
           For whom, and not for Tybalt, Juliet pin'd.
           You, to remove that siege of grief from her,
           Betroth'd and would have married her perforce
           To County Paris. Then comes she to me,
240   And with wild looks bid me devise some mean
           To rid her from this second marriage,
           Or in my cell there would she kill herself.
           Then gave I her (so tutor'd by my art)
           A sleeping potion, which so took effect
245   As I intended, for it wrought on her
           The form of death. Mean time I writ to Romeo
           That he should hither come as this dire night
           To help to take her from her borrow'd grave,

---

210 my liege my lord

214 untaught Montague scolds Romeo for dying before his father has taught him how by example.

216 mouth of outrage cries of anguish

219 general of your woes your leader in seeking justice

220 even to death even to seeking a death sentence

220 forbear be patient

221 let mischance be slave to patience let misfortune be ruled by patience

223 greatest prime suspect

225 make accuse; speak

226 impeach and purge accuse and acquit

229 my short date of breath my brief remaining life

233 stol'n secret

236 pin'd grieved

238 perforce by force

243 tutor'd by my art guided by my knowledge of herbs

246 form appearance

247 as on

Being the time the potion's force should cease.
250 But he which bore my letter, Friar John,
Was stay'd by accident, and yesternight
Return'd my letter back. Then all alone,
At the prefixed hour of her waking,
Came I to take her from her kindred's vault,
255 Meaning to keep her closely at my cell,
Till I conveniently could send to Romeo.
But when I came, some minute ere the time
Of her awakening, here untimely lay
The noble Paris and true Romeo dead.
260 She wakes, and I entreated her come forth
And bear this work of heaven with patience.
But then a noise did scare me from the tomb,
And she too desperate would not go with me,
But as it seems, did violence on herself.
265 All this I know, and to the marriage
Her nurse is privy; and if aught in this
Miscarried by my fault, let my old life
Be sacrific'd, some hour before his time,
Unto the rigour of severest law.

270 PRINCE We still have known thee for a holy man.
Where's Romeo's man? what can he say to this?

BALTHASAR I brought my master news of Juliet's death,
And then in post he came from Mantua
To this same place, to this same monument.
275 This letter he early bid me give his father,
And threaten'd me with death, going in the vault,
If I departed not and left him there.

PRINCE Give me the letter, I will look on it.
Where is the County's page that rais'd the Watch?
280 Sirrah, what made your master in this place?

PAGE He came with flowers to strew his lady's grave,
And bid me stand aloof, and so I did.
Anon comes one with light to ope the tomb,
And by and by my master drew on him,
285 And then I ran away to call the Watch.

PRINCE This letter doth make good the Friar's words,
Their course of love, the tidings of her death;
And here he writes that he did buy a poison
Of a poor pothecary, and therewithal

251 **stay'd** delayed
255 **closely** secretly
261 **bear this work of heaven** accept this situation
266 **is privy** is aware
266 **aught** anything
267 **Miscarried** went wrong
270 **still** always
273 **in post** quickly
280 **made** did
283 **Anon** soon
283 **ope** open
286 **make good** confirm
289 **therewithal** with the poison

290   Came to this vault to die, and lie with Juliet.
        Where be these enemies? Capulet, Montague?
        See what a scourge is laid upon your hate,
        That heaven finds means to kill your joys with love!
        And I for winking at your discords too
295   Have lost a brace of kinsmen. All are punish'd.

CAPULET   O brother Montague, give me thy hand.
        This is my daughter's jointure, for no more
        Can I demand.

MONTAGUE   But I can give thee more,
        For I will raise her statue in pure gold,
300   That whiles Verona by that name is known,
        There shall no figure at such rate be set
        As that of true and faithful Juliet.

CAPULET   As rich shall Romeo's by his lady's lie,
        Poor sacrifices of our enmity!

305 PRINCE   A glooming peace this morning with it brings,
        The sun for sorrow will not show his head.
        Go hence to have more talk of these sad things;
        Some shall be pardon'd, and some punished:
        For never was a story of more woe
310   Than this of Juliet and her Romeo.   [*Exeunt omnes*

---

294 for winking at your discords for turning a blind eye to your conflicts

295 brace of kinsmen pair of relatives (i.e., Mercutio and Paris)

297 jointure Money traditionally paid to a wife on the death of her husband.

301 at such rate be set that will be held in such high esteem

305 glooming gloomy

310 s.d. Exeunt omnes all exit

Notes